D0414603

AI

BENNY ANDERSEN

Benny Andersen, 1978. Photography by Gregers Nielsen, courtesy of Borgens Forlag, Publishers.

BENNY ANDERSEN
A Critical Study

LEONIE MARX

Contributions to the Study of World Literature, Number 1

GREENWOOD PRESS
Westport, Connecticut • London, England

Library of Congress Cataloging in Publication Data

Marx, Leonie.
    Benny Andersen, a critical study.

    (Contributions to the study of world literature,
ISSN 0738-9345 ; no. 1)
    Bibliography: p.
    Includes index.
    1. Andersen, Benny—Criticism and interpretation.
I. Title.   II. Series.
PT8176.1.N56Z77   1983   839.8'187409   83-12945
ISBN 0-313-24168-6 (lib. bdg.)

This investigation was supported by University of Kansas General Research allocation 3480-x9-0038.

Selections from *Benny Andersen: Selected Poems,* translated by Alexander Taylor, copyright © 1975 by Princeton University Press, are reprinted by permission of Princeton University Press. Certain of the translations which appear in this book first appeared in *Seventeen Danish Poets,* published by Windflower Press.

Copyright © 1983 by Leonie Marx

All rights reserved. No portion of this book may be
reproduced, by any process or technique, without the
express written consent of the publisher.

Library of Congress Catalog Card Number: 83-12945
ISBN: 0-313-24168-6
ISSN: 0738-9345

First published in 1983

Greenwood Press
A division of Congressional Information Service, Inc.
88 Post Road West, Westport, Connecticut 06881

Printed in the United States of America

10 9 8 7 6 5 4 3 2 1

"The realization that life is absurd cannot be an end in itself but only a beginning. It is a truth which nearly all great minds have taken as their starting point. It is not this discovery which is interesting, but the consequences and the rules for action which can be drawn from it."

Albert Camus*

Contents

About the Author

Leonie Marx is an Associate Professor of Germanic Languages and Literatures at the University of Kansas, where she has taught in the fields of German and Scandinavian since 1976. She received her Ph.D. from the University of Illinois and held a position in Scandinavian Studies at the University of Wisconsin. Her publications include a variety of articles on modern Danish literature, on German literature of the nineteenth and twentieth centuries and on German-Danish literary relations. A volume of selected short stories by Benny Andersen in English translation with her critical introduction was published in 1983.

Preface

    As one of the most popular representatives of contemporary
Danish literature, Benny Andersen has transcended language barriers and has become increasingly known abroad through translations of his poetry and short fiction into several languages. In
1975 Princeton University Press published a major selection of his
poetry in English translation, and a volume, <u>Selected Stories</u>, has
been published by Curbstone Press. This representative cross-
section of Andersen's narrative works to date contains the stories
"Hiccups," "Layer Cake," "The Pants" (from <u>The Pillows</u>), and "Fats
Olsen," "A Happy Fellow" (from <u>Fats Olsen and Other Stories</u>), as
well as a key chapter, "The Speaking Strike," from Andersen's
first novel <u>On the Bridge</u> (1981). The author's sense of humor,
which often borders on the grotesque, his acute observation of social dynamics, and his psychological insight into the human personality are combined in a sharp focus on the dark side of human
conduct. In keeping with an early, self-imposed challenge to
"spit out/ even if stains should get on existence," Andersen has
developed a unique style in modern Danish literature.
    Within the modern literary tradition, he has contributed to
the understanding of social dynamics in everyday life by his
close-up views of the individual's difficulties and traumas in our
Western, technologically advanced society. While his humorous
portrayals of human types and typical situations have contributed
greatly to the enthusiastic reception of Andersen's poems and
short stories, they have overshadowed to a degree the serious
dimension in his works, for even though Andersen's social
criticism has been recognized, it has usually not been linked to
the motivating ideas and thematic pattern underlying his <u>oeuvre</u>.
Only a few literary critics have hinted at Andersen's dialectical
pattern of thought, and thus an analytical study of his works is
still lacking, even in Denmark. It is therefore the aim of this

monograph to investigate the unifying thematic foundation for Andersen's writing and to identify its ethical component, as well as
to discuss the characteristics of his literary strategy. The
analysis will focus on Andersen's poetry and fiction, which
established his reputation as a Modernist writer. Andersen's
plays and books for children, although they merit a more detailed
treatment, can only be discussed briefly in the framework of this
study.

It will be pointed out, however, that there is a close connection between Benny Andersen's books for children and his other
works. In this respect, the Snøvsen-trilogy constitutes a
veritable guide to meaningful social interaction, because seeing
the other person--not merely in a particular social role but also
as a more complex person wanting to live a full life--is practiced
by the children. Benny Andersen cleverly manages to include both
adults and children in his model world by choosing as the main
character "snøvs," a phantastic little creature he invented on the
basis of an idiom. While snøvs lives in a world of his own
dreams, fears, errors, and good intentions, his unconventional
perspective underscores the complexity of life while also trans-
mitting psychological insight into human behavior. Andersen thus
presents an approach to daily interaction usually depicted in his
other works as lacking in contemporary society and, at the same
time, he demonstrates in his children's books that his popular innovative word play goes well beyond a joy in linguistic games, for
it serves to communicate his ethical concerns.

Chapter One of the study provides a chronological overview of
Andersen's literary production until 1981. Besides discussing the
major literary and historical developments in Denmark as they
relate to Andersen's position as a writer, it complements the in
depth treatment of specific thematic and structural characteristics which follows in the remainder of the book. Chapter Two
concentrates entirely on Andersen's first collection of poetry,
The Musical Eel (1960), because its poems cover a time span of
nearly a decade and reveal essential points of departure for Andersen's works, including genres other than poetry. In the following chapters, Andersen's major poems are given detailed attention according to the basic pattern discernable in the nine
volumes of poetry he has published to date. This study concludes
with an investigation of his fictional works, including his first
novel On the Bridge (1981), which he made available in manuscript
form for this monograph.

For assistance in the preparation of this critical introduction, I should like to thank the following institutions: the Royal
Library in Copenhagen, with special thanks to the research
librarian, Jesper During Jørgensen, for his prompt assistance in
procuring materials; to Danmarks Radio, for providing the film
version of the story "Fats Olsen," and to the University of Kansas
for its generous support through a research allocation and the
Small Grants Fund. I am especially grateful to the author, Benny
Andersen, and to his wife Cynthia Bramsen for their cooperation
and discussions; to the publisher Jarl Borgen for allowing me to
use his archives; to Professor Niels Ingwersen for his critical
reading of this manuscript, and to Professor Leif Sjöberg for his

advice as editor of this Scandinavian Series. Above all, I am in-
debted to L. C. Marx, and to Professors Barbara and Frank Lide for
their most generous editorial assistance in preparing the final
version of this book. I should also like to thank the following
publishers for granting me permission to quote from Andersen's
works: Borgens Forlag, Copenhagen, for the right to translate
from the Danish originals; Princeton University Press, for quotations from Selected Poems; and Windflower Press, for quotations
from Seventeen Danish Poets.

LEONIE MARX

University of Kansas

Chronology

1929   Benny Allan Andersen born November 7 in the Copenhagen
        suburb of Søborg.
1940   April 9, Denmark is occupied by German troops.
1942   Andersen begins taking piano lessons.
1943   Graduates from Bakkegårdskolen.
1944   June 26 until July 5, the citizens of Copenhagen protest
        against the German occupation with a general strike and
        street barricades; while attending night school, Andersen
        works at various jobs: as a messenger boy in a grocery
        store and in an engineering firm, subsequently in an ad-
        vertising agency.
1945   May 5, the German occupation ends as Denmark is liberated
        by Allied forces.
1948   Andersen completes night school and receives his high
        school graduation certificate; the literary-cultural jour-
        nal Heretica is founded.
1949   Andersen leaves the advertising agency and begins working
        as a bar pianist in Esbjerg on the Danish West coast.
1950   Marries Signe Plesner, graphic artist; starts travelling
        as a pianist through Danish provincial towns; daughter
        Lisbet is born.
1952-   Andersen's first poems appear in Heretica before the jour-
1953   nal ceases publication; as a member of a trio of musi-
        cians, he travels through Denmark, Norway and Sweden.
1957   Son Kim is born; Andersen starts publishing his poems in
        Hvedekorn.
1958-   Travels with his trio to New York aboard a Norwegian ocean
1959   liner; visits Minton's Playhouse in Harlem.
1960   Beginning of anti-nuclear arms rallies in and around
        Copenhagen; Andersen's first collection of poetry,

Den musikalske ål (The Musical Eel) is published by Borgen; new poems appear in Vindrosen and Hvedekorn; Andersen
settles with his family in Copenhagen and works as a bar
pianist in a night-café in the Frederiksberg section of
town.

1962   The second collection of poetry, Kamera med køkkenadgang
(Camera with Kitchen Privileges), is published; Andersen
stops working as a bar pianist.

1963   Collects and edits Danish nursery rhymes, Nikke Nikke Nambo.

1963-   During the winter season, Andersen plays the piano for the
1964   Fiol Theater's program in Copenhagen.

1964   Collects and edits foreign nursery rhymes, Lille
Peter Dille (Little Peter Dille); publishes the collection
of poetry, Den indre bowlerhat   (The Inner Bowler Hat);
receives the Louisiana award.

1965   Andersen's first collection of short stories, Puderne
(The Pillows), appears, and the radio play Snak (Talk), as
well as the record "Benny Andersen læser Benny Andersen"
("Benny Andersen reads Benny Andersen"); is awarded the
cultural prize of the workers' union and the Carl Møller
stipend for humorists.

1966   Receives the Danish critics' prize; publishes the poem
"Kæmperne" ("The Warriors") in the international anthology
Ord om Vietnam (Words about Vietnam) which he also co-
edits; publishes the volume of poetry Portrætgalleri (Portrait Gallery).

1967   Publishes Snøvsen og Eigil og katten i sækken (Snøvsen and
Eigil and the Cat in the Bag), a book for children.

1968   Tykke-Olsen m.fl.   (Fats Olsen and Other Stories), Andersen's second collection of short stories appears.

1969   Den hæse drage (The Hoarse Dragon), a comedy for children,
is presented as a book and as a record; the radio play
Lejemorderen (The Hired Assassin) and the volume of
poetry, Det sidste øh (The Last Er), appear.

1970   The collection of radio and TV plays Lejemorderen og andre spil   (The Hired Assassin and Other Plays) is published, and the children's book Snøvsen på sommerferie
(Snøvsen on Summer Vacation).

1971   Andersen is awarded the prize for juvenile books given by
the Ministry for Cultural Affairs; an anthology of his
poems covering the period of 1960-69 is edited by the
scholar and critic Niels Barfoed under the title
Man burde burde (You Oughta Oughta); the collection of
poetry   Her i reservatet   (Here on the Reserve)   is
published.

1972   Elected to the Danish Academy; publishes the children's
book Snøvsen og Snøvsine (Snøvsen and Snøvsine), the film
script   Man sku' være noget ved musikken   (You Oughta Be
Somebody; with Henning Carlsen), and the tale Svantes viser (Svante's Songs); he sets the poems in Svante's Songs to music, which is later recorded by the singer
Povl Dissing; Andersen contributes the story "Die
lebensgefährlichen Tulpen" ("The Deadly Tulips") to the

international anthology Dichter Europas erzählen Kindern (European Writers Tell Stories to Children); Denmark joins the European Common Market.

1973   In collaboration with children, Andersen writes and records the novel for radio Undskyld hr.-- hvor ligger naturen? (Excuse me, Sir-- where is Nature?); also publishes the volume of essays and reminiscences Barnet der blev ældre og ældre (The Child Who Grew Older and Older).

1974   Receives the Hans Christian Andersen stipend; contributes the essay "Børns sprog og børns oplevelse af sproget" ("Children's Language and Children's Experience of Language") to the book on language published by the Danish Academy; another collection of poetry, Personlige papirer (Personal Papers), appears; makes the film (with Henning Carlsen) Da Svante forsvandt (When Svante disappeared).

1975   Is awarded the bookdealer's prize "The Golden Laurel" and the Otto Rung stipend for writers; presents the film script En lykkelig skilsmisse (A Happy Divorce) together with Henning Carlsen.

1976   Publishes a volume of poems and reminiscences, Nomader med noder (Nomads with Notes).

1977   Andersen and his wife Signe separate.

1978   The collection of poetry Under begge øjne (Under Both Eyes) is published; the play Orfeus i undergrunden (Orpheus in the Underground) is broadcast on Danish radio;

1979   it was adapted for the stage a year later; the collection of poems, Himmelspræt eller kunsten at komme til verden (Blanket-Toss or the Art of Coming into the World) appears.

1979-   Presents the play Kolde fødder (Cold Feet) for the theater
1980   season.

1980   With Dan Tschernia, he prepares the film script for Orpheus in the Underground under the title Danmark er lukket (Denmark is Closed); together with Povl Dissing, the singer of Svante's Songs, Andersen receives the award of the International Federation of Producers of Phonograms and Videograms.

1981   Andersen is granted a stipend by the San Cataldo Foundation; presents his first novel På broen (On the Bridge); the song book and the record (with Povl Dissing) Oven visse vande (Above Certain Waters) appear; contributes the essay "Notater om inspiration" ("Notes about Inspiration") to the book on inspiration published by the Danish Academy; subsequent to his divorce from Signe Plesner Andersen, he marries Cynthia Bramsen.

1983   Andersen tours the United States, reading from his works; his visit is a part of the "Scandinavia Today" program, a series of cultural events designed to familiarize Americans with modern Scandinavian culture.

BENNY ANDERSEN

1

Phases of Development

Benny Andersen's poetic universe opens to the reader an immensely colorful but enigmatically dissonant portrait of modern society revolving around the axis of a first person speaker. With his depictions of individual struggles and assumed social roles, Andersen directs a critical perspective to the attempts of both the individual and society at silencing existential and social dissonance. An affinity with Kafka is clearly visible in the futile efforts of Andersen's negative heroes who try to cope with the anonymity in society and the overwhelming demands of an everyday life whose meaning remains an enigma to them. By pointing to the substitutes devised daily as compensation for the absence of an unequivocal meaning of life, Andersen breaks through facades and uncovers an often rigid power struggle among people or within the individual. As a contemporary social critic and moralist, he can be said to carry on in the spirit of such Scandinavian authors as Kierkegaard, Ibsen, and Strindberg. The reasons for Andersen's popularity in Denmark and abroad lie in his focus on everyday problems surrounding the average person and in his tragicomic strategy for putting those problems at a distance. But his comic portrayals should not detract from the impressive thematic and structural complexity of his work, which is based on the variations of a few major themes and must be seen in the context of the modern literary tradition, with specific attention given to Danish cultural developments after World War II.

I Formative Years

Andersen was born on November 7, 1929, in the Copenhagen
suburb of Søborg. His formative years regarding his personal
ethics, coincide with a time of historical upheaval, with that
phase of World War II which affected Denmark directly on account
of the German occupation from 1940 until 1945. In his work, the
traces of this time can be found in a concern about the roots of
Fascism in everyday life. In the short stories, they are seen in
the ruthlessly egocentric power struggle or the intolerance toward
those who differ from the norm and are exposed to a "lynch mentality;" in the poems, they are visible in a concern about the
one-sided admiration for the "strong man"[1] or about a blind, self-
righteous judging of others, as in "The Hanged Informer."[2] He did
not take up this period directly, however, until 1981, when he
wrote his first novel, On the Bridge (På broen), a portrayal of
individual ethical development against the background of
historical events.

For Andersen personally, the 1940's were decisive years. As
the eldest of four children of a bricklayer, he had to leave
school at the age of thirteen to help support his family. A year
before, his family had purchased a piano by installments and he
was given lessons by his father's cousin. His interest for the
piano continued after he had left school. Working as a messenger
boy for a cheese store, and subsequently for a factory producing
radiator meters, he attended night school and received his high
school graduation certificate in 1948. Although he had started an
office career in an advertising firm, he soon decided to follow up
his musical talent instead and began as a bar pianist in Esbjerg
on the Danish West coast. It was at this time, around 1948, that
Andersen first became interested in lyric poetry, an interest
promoted in part by Signe Plesner, a graphic artist he had met in
night school and whom he married in 1950. Signe had a deep interest in poetry and encouraged him in his early attempts. Also,
poetry was the dominant genre in Danish literature during the
1940's and well beyond, causing heated debates among Danish intellectuals.

The literary situation in Denmark, especially during the
1940's, cannot be viewed detached from the historical situation.
Since the German occupation had brought enforced isolation to Denmark, an already relatively self-contained culture whose own
literary tradition had been the focal point until 1940, Danish intellectuals realized the need to redefine their position; consequently, they made efforts to break out of their cultural isolation and gain access to the main currents of world literature.
The aesthetics of Symbolism, which had spread across Europe at the
turn of the century, became dominant in poetry, while narrative
art followed mainly the persisting tradition of Realism. Of the
two eminent dramatists at the time--Kjeld Abell (1901-1961) and
Kaj Munk (1898-1944)--Abell was the only innovative playwright.[3]

Literary and sociopolitical questions were brought closer
together through the events of World War II. Both the horrors
revealed after the war and the onset of a cold war had sharpened

the awareness of Danish intellectuals concerning threatened
humanistic values. In intense discussions, they adhered to the
ethics of the resistance movement--to guarantee human rights and
to improve society. Based on this orientation, they demanded a
new beginning in society as well as in literature after the
liberation in 1945. Although the younger generation--to a higher
degree than the already established writers like H. C. Branner
(1903-1966), Martin A. Hansen (1909-1955), Erik Knudsen (b. 1922),
Paul la Cour (1902-1956), and Ole Wivel (b. 1921)--reacted with
utmost skepticism to the value systems of any existing ideologies,
they were willing to participate in the shaping of a new
beginning. The question which received foremost attention in
regard to this new start was about the role of artists and intellectuals, specifically with respect to their responsibility in a
sociopolitical framework. Two opposing answers came from the
circles of two competing literary-cultural journals, Heretica and
Dialog. Defending Heretica's so-called ideologically independent
position, Ole Wivel argued that poetry by nature was protection
against ideological ossification.[4] His opponents in this debate
were associated with the leftist-oriented journal Dialog
(1950-61),[5] which continued in the vein of its predecessor
Athenæum and demanded a clearcut social involvement in current
problems, arguing that politics was applied ethics.[6] They based
their demand on Jean-Paul Sartre's call for social involvement on
the part of the writer through participation in social activity,
such as the peace movement.[7] In spite of strongly conflicting
opinions among writers, they all started off from the same basic
premises, namely, that a repetition of past cruelties had to be
prevented by working for detente on an international level, and
that a literary mode of expression had to be found that corresponded to contemporary problems.

In this transitional situation between traditional values and
new ones that needed to be formulated, Martin A. Hansen observed
what he called ethical pessimism in the younger generation. He
recognized a skeptical attitude toward the ideological prejudice
that the young writers encountered in existing values. He saw
this as symptomatic of the human dichotomy and isolation and of
the literary fragmentation prevalent in European culture on the
whole. An outgrowth of this development, according to Hansen, was
the preference of the younger writers to renew the short, strin-
gently composed literary forms: drama, lyric poetry, and the
short story--especially the last two; and here, it was the poetry
of Symbolism that dominated, promoted by the writers associated
with Heretica. Their creed can be summed up in the key phrase
"emancipation of the image;" they believed that the chaos of the
world could still be transcended by poetry--that is, by the creation of an individual poetic world in which antithetical elements
could be brought together in a unifying symbol.[8] Although Heretica
ceased publication in 1953, while it was deeply entrenched in a
controversy about the cryptic and obscure poetic model it
propagated, the journal had set the tone for modern Danish poetry.
Benny Andersen's first poems were also published in Heretica in
the two years before it was replaced by the newly founded Vindrosen. These early poems reflect an affinity with Heretica's in-

troverted, Symbolistic orientation, and with Rilke, whose poetry was represented in Heretica and had inspired "The Forgotten Son" ("Den glemte søn").[9]

During the 1950's, when Andersen published his first poems in Danish journals, he was travelling as a pianist throughout the Danish province after leaving his job in Esbjerg. After he had formed a trio with two other musicians, his tours were expanded to Sweden and Norway, where the trio played in resort hotels on the coasts and in the mountains for a period of four years. In 1958, an engagement on a Norwegian ocean liner brought the group all the way to New York and to Minton's Playhouse in Harlem, a celebrated jazz club in the 1940's. An impression from this visit is reflected in Andersen's poem "Thelonious Monk."[10]

That Andersen's nomadic life, spanning the entire decade of the 1950's, was an adventurous but hardly glamorous undertaking, is apparent from the poems and anecdotes he published about those years.[11] During that time, Italian pop music was favored in Denmark and along with it were favored Italian musicians who played for lower rates. When Danish musicians side-stepped the problem by moving on to Norway, their competition with Norwegian musicians triggered a veritable migration of musicians through Scandinavia. Benny Andersen's choice of such an irregular life as opposed to that he led at the advertising agency attests to his interest in expanding his experiences with people beyond the Danish horizon. It corresponds to a philosophy of life which emerges in his poetry later on and stresses the necessity to keep on moving--that is, to keep developing mentally and not settle in a fixed, often provincial, outlook on life. Having chosen an improvised life-style filled with not always pleasant surprises, yet with a wealth of inspirations, Andersen voiced his affirmative attitude toward it: "We travel around / our life is to travel / we travel to live."[12] Both in an economic and in a philosophical sense, the necessities of life merge here, expressing the commitment to meet the challenge of the factual situation by exploring the freedom it entails: the ambiguous freedom of the travelling artist.

On the longer tours through Scandinavia, Andersen's wife and their two children--their daughter Lisbet and their son Kim-- accompanied him as long as it did not interfere with the children's schooling. But in 1960 the family settled in Copenhagen, where Andersen started as a bar pianist in a night-café in the Frederiksberg section of town. By then he had not only published poems in Heretica, but also in Vindrosen and in Hvedekorn, a journal in which many Danish authors made their literary debut. While Heretica's influence had gradually subsided throughout the 1950's, Andersen too, was developing an independent style, as indicated by his brief poetic glimpses of nature published in Hvedekorn at the end of the 1950's. On the basis of these poems, he was discovered by the Copenhagen publisher Jarl Borgen, with the result that in 1960, his first collection of poetry appeared, The Musical Eel (Den musikalske ål). Since the initial acknowledgement of Andersen as a lyrical poet is closely connected with the journal Heretica, it is no secret that his early literary inspiration is linked to the European Symbolist tradition. Andersen himself has pointed out Rilke, Baudelaire, and Rimbaud, as well as the Danish

poet Paul la Cour in this respect.[13] In addition, he had become
acquainted with the works of Swedish, especially Finno-Swedish,
poets on his tours to Sweden. The complexity of lyrical expression he met in their poems, in the disquieting quality of Edith
Södergran's poetic images, for instance, stimulated his interest
in poetry during the 1950's.[14]

Most of the poems in his first collection reveal what might
be called an uncanny dimension of life that is often placed at a
distance through humor, especially in the short fables from nature's micro-society. But it is in the last four long prose poems
that this dimension is most intensely felt as an all pervasive
threat to existence. This threat is made exceptionally clear
through metaphoric and mimetic depiction of a cultural environment
so easily identifiable as our own. As the threat culminates, it
reflects the existential insecurity prevalent throughout the
1950's and well into the new decade owing partly to the cold war
atmosphere. This sense of danger was paralleled by the internal
and world-wide development of growing industrialization and an expanding consumer attitude which had even more direct and concrete
effects on individual lives. When The Musical Eel appeared in
1960, this feeling of immediate and world-wide threat was
beginning to consolidate and was soon finding expression in the
anti-nuclear arms marches on Copenhagen in 1961 and subsequent
years. It is therefore not surprising that security turns out to
be a key theme for Andersen, a security which was being administered on an increasing scale by the Danish welfare state, yet
was lacking profoundly on an individual, national, and international level. That Andersen grew up at a time when ethical
questions intensely occupied public debates and often focused on
the author's role in society can be sensed in the volume's last
four prose poems. The complexity of this theme in Andersen's work
is suggested by Niels Barfoed's term "security psychosis" in a
very perceptive review of The Musical Eel.[15]

What is implied precisely by pointing to our "security psychosis" is explored by Andersen in his scrutinizing closeups of
everyday life with its apparently well integrated problems. His
psychological insight discloses many of the interlocking aspects
of personal insecurity, primarily the substitutions made for the
lack of security, their futility, or even their detrimental effects on people and interpersonal relationships. The imperative
of having to take a stand is at least partly if not directly
visible in Andersen's subsequent works, for which this first
volume, with its ethical and literary aims, forms a basis. Most
critics have overlooked this last point, however, since the prose
poems were usually dismissed as being comparatively inferior.[16]
Although their thematic intensification leads to an abundance of
associations that require a more unified structural organization,
their stated and implied goals do constitute an essential point of
departure for Andersen's literary production.

II   Facets of an Ongoing Production

Following up on themes and structural techniques from The Musical Eel, Andersen developed a poetic style that also became characteristic for his later work in other genres. He continued to offer his poems to Hvedekorn and also, increasingly, to Vindrosen, which at the beginning of the 1960's was becoming the mouthpiece for a younger generation of writers extremely concerned with the decreasing quality of life in an environment marked by international tension, social taboos, and superficial values. Vindrosen's two prominent editors at this time were the authors Klaus Rifbjerg (b. 1931) and Villy Sørensen (b. 1929). Sørensen, in his complex role as author, philosopher, and literary and social critic, formulated the younger generation's uneasiness about an externally well insured life which, rather than protect against the repressed collective traumas about continuous dangers and uncertainties, actually promoted them.[17]

The poems Andersen published after 1960 were included in his second collection. When it appeared in 1962, it signalled his transition from the brief lyrical fables to everyday portraits of human types and attitudes. While keeping the technique that he developed in the fables, he now expanded it at the linguistic level. In The Musical Eel, the unusual focus of a subjective impression could lead to the reversal of natural laws and thus project an expanded awareness: "The sun has stopped / in front of a singing lark."[18] This technique is increasingly applied to the verbal material in the second volume, Camera with Kitchen Privileges (Kamera med køkkenadgang) in which a perspective that contrasts with wide-spread norms is achieved by changing around common idioms: "children of unwanted parents" is one such example.[19] Here, Andersen's play upon the idiom creates an awareness of the darker side of everyday life and, as the collection's title indicates, of the situation of the less privileged. By defamiliarizing normative speaking habits and thus altering an established focus on society, Andersen injects into his poems that disquieting quality he admired in Edith Södergran's poetic images.

After the publication of his second book, Andersen gave up his job as a bar pianist to devote himself entirely to his literary interests; he played again during the winters of 1963 and 1964 but then only for programs at the Fiol Theater, a prestigious avant-garde stage in Copenhagen. With his third collection of poetry in 1964, The Inner Bowlerhat (Den indre bowlerhat), he consolidated the recognition he had received so far as a modern Danish poet with a distinct stylistic technique and a unique sense of humor. While the satirical mode of the previous volume continued, Andersen focused increasingly on the complexity of life as it daily confronts the individual. Not so much individual powerlessness is emphasized here, but rather the necessity to activate individual potential in our concern with life and happiness. Inhibitions must be overcome, and "the inner Bowler hat" has to be swallowed; the risks of being here and now must be taken, and individual awareness needs to be expanded. Andersen's concern with the importance of awareness determines his thematic and structural perspectives. Also, his experimentation with idiomatic expressions must be seen as directly related to this concern. A humorous twist at the verbal level placed into a serious context accounts for his range of humor from the ironic to the grotesque.

With his interest in word play, Andersen discovered his affinity to children's playful treatment of language.[20] He began collecting Danish nursery rhymes and translated a number of foreign rhymes, which led to the publications of Nikke Nikke Nambo (1963) and Little Peter Dille (Lille Peter Dille, 1964).[21] Andersen was not alone with his interest in children's unconventional use of language. Hans Magnus Enzensberger's well known anthology of German rhymes had appeared in the early 1960's,[22] and by the middle of the decade, concrete poets had not only revived Dadaist experiments with language but also appreciated the candid and frolicsome use of language that they observed among children. This can especially be seen in the vivid experiments of Vagn Steen, a leading poet in the Danish concrete poetry movement. Andersen did not, however, go as far as those concrete poets who limited themselves to typographical experimentation at the expense of the sound level.[23] In his own literary word play, he sometimes includes an unconventional typographical arrangement in a poem; but it functions chiefly to underscore thematic complexity, as he depicts desperate, often tragicomic and futile efforts to cope with life in a modern progress-oriented society. With his focus on everyday life, the discrepancies between ideal and reality and his close-ups of the so-called common man, Andersen transmits his view of universal human problems, along with the difficulties characteristic of our highly industrialized environment.

In his subsequent volumes of poetry, he also varies a small number of major themes, expanding them and demonstrating their complexity by means of his detailed perception of our surroundings. He does this by placing different key motifs in the center of each volume. In Portrait Gallery (Portrætgalleri) of 1966, there is a visible emphasis on the necessity to keep on moving if stagnation is to be avoided. In addition to self-development, the necessity to reach out and communicate is strikingly formulated in the poem "This Is" ("Her er"), which reflects the nursery rhyme "This Is the House that Jack Built" ("Her er det hus som Jakob bygged"). The motif of communication is a key aspect of Andersen's main theme of authentic balance in life. This is clearly expressed in The Last Er (Det sidste øh, 1969), in which Andersen takes a close look at the poet in society. Here Andersen's dialectical pattern of thought and expression is prominently formulated in "Toddler" ("Tumling"), with a clever usage of juxtaposed active and passive forms of Danish verbs. This poem can justly be considered a continuation of "This Is,"[24] since the motif of balancing serves as a link between them.

With Here on the Reserve (Her i reservatet) in 1971, Andersen presented a polemically outspoken volume, composed in a dialectical pattern. The first section, "Reports from the Reserve" presents the outside observer's point of view, while the second, "Voices from the Reserve" gives the inhabitants' inside perspective. Both the observer and the member of this endangered human species "On the Reserve," focus on the paradoxical behavior of humans, which reveals a misconception of the priorities they have chosen. In contrast to the contemporary views of the first two sections, the third section--a long prose poem on "Daily Life on the Reserve in the Twentieth Century"--is written from the retrospective of a historiographer looking at old photographs in the year 2071. Here, it is clear that the historiographer's selection of pictures is taken from Danish life, because the poem starts with the first line from the Danish national anthem in the style of a fairy tale beginning: "There was a lovely country" ("Der var et yndigt land"). The poem reads like a nostalgic description of a by-gone Golden Age when it was possible to develop through personal choice. It presents a genre-picture of Danish life in the second half of the twentieth century whose eighteenth century literary antecedents inevitably come to mind, for instance Goethe's Hermann und Dorothea. [25] In the case of Andersen's genre-picture, there is a tongue-in-cheek speaker whose perspective functions like the eye of a camera when moving from one photograph to the next. The poem culminates with the historiographer's self-definition, which is characteristic of Andersen's dialectical thought pattern. His selection of contrasting impressions is to be understood as a "bound person's free choice" in the year 2071. Besides raising the question of what may have happened to that "lovely country" and what the historiographer's environment might be like, the poem stresses with its ending Andersen's theme that individual potential has to be realized and developed. Similarly, the entire volume, with its emphasis on the process of mutual influence between individual and society, and society and environment, recalls Andersen's proclamation from The Musical Eel, that we are the environment.

Also, the added political dimension of Here on the Reserve cannot pass unmentioned. While it gave a critical view of Danish society, the book also conveyed the possibility of outside intervention into Danish affairs and a deep concern about Denmark's future. At a time when documentary writing was becoming prominent, the book was received by Danish critics as the first serious literary contribution to the ongoing political debate over the question of Denmark joining the European Common Market.[26]

After Denmark joined the European Economic Community in 1972, Andersen's opposition to this membership became even more evident in his play Orpheus in the Underground (Orfeus i undergrunden, 1978), which shows that this membership has resulted in the extinction of the Danish state. Based on the play, Andersen and the film maker Dan Tschernia, wrote the script for the film entitled Denmark Is Closed (Danmark er lukket, 1980).

During the 1960's, Andersen wrote some radio plays in which he used the absurd to depict individual self-assertion (Talk; Snak, 1965), and in which a satirical focus is placed on society (The Hired Assassin and Other Plays; Lejemorderen og andre spil, 1970). He continued his dramatic work with a couple of film-scripts in the 1970's and, most recently, with a play for the theater, Cold Feet (Kolde fødder, 1980) which centers on a woman's difficulties with social norms;[27] here, as in his most recent poetry, Andersen presents love as a key to overcoming obstacles.

Simultaneously, Andersen's interest in children's language and their less "normalized" perspective of their surroundings led to further books for children. They are structured around a phantastic little creature, snøvs, whose name is derived from a Danish idiom meaning "to lose one's head." Fixed, one-sided perspectives are exposed by snøvs with the help of the children.

In Andersen's prose works of the mid to late 1960's, we can recognize a specific line of development which is related to that in his poetry. When his two collections of short stories appeared, The Pillows (Puderne) in 1965 and Fats Olsen and Other Stories (Tykke-Olsen m.fl.)in 1968, the trend in Danish prose had undergone a significant change from the tradition of Realism that had been dominant throughout the 1940's. Primarily two authors, Peter Seeberg, (b. 1925) and Villy Sørensen (b. 1929), were credited with having initiated the turn to a "Modernistic" Danish prose literature in the early 1950's. In their short stories, they had introduced the absurd and the phantastic as encountered by people in a modern impersonal society. Andersen's stories, especially those in the first volume, reveal an affinity with the absurd. He seems to concentrate on extreme attitudes more in his stories than in his poems. This impression is called forth because uncommon, if not deviant behavior is seen within the context of a familiar, everyday situation and appears alarmingly out of proportion. Each volume is composed with a thematic coherence. While the second collection builds on the motifs familiar from The Pillows, it directs the reader's attention more to social norms. With a subdivision into two sections, "Outside" as opposed to "Inside," meaning in this case outside or inside of marriage, these stories probe into the frustrated, unhappy lives of their protagonists, demonstrating the fundamental similarity between the problems of married and unmarried people.

During the 1970's, Andersen's works reveal an additional tendency: he now speaks more directly about his own life instead of hiding behind portraits of types and attitudes. A collection of essays published in 1973, The Child that Grew Older and Older (Barnet der blev ældre og ældre), was followed in 1976 by a volume of poems, diary entries, and prose sketches from his years as a travelling musician, Nomads with Notes (Nomader med noder). In the interim Svante's Songs (Svantes viser, 1972)--a longer narrative with interspersed poems set to music, composed by Andersen himself--became an enormous success. In 1974 a collection of poetry appeared, Personal Papers (Personlige papirer), thematically grouped around the experiences of emptiness. Andersen's code of ethics and his hope to bridge emptiness with warmth and meaningful contact with others are more directly formulated here. He seems to open himself more to the reader in accordance with his demand to open up not only eyes but also open up as a person when interacting with others. This trend continues in the most recent collections of poetry, Under Both Eyes (Under begge øjne, 1978) and Blanket-Toss or the Art of Coming into the World (Himmelspræt eller Kunsten at komme til verden, 1979). The poems are no longer packed with images, symbols and word plays in a dramatic associative rhythm leading up to a final effect. As the symbolic titles indicate, significant structural and thematic features of his work are emerging more clearly in these volumes. Andersen's associative technique is directed toward exploring a theme by means of its numerous positive and negative aspects, rather than on the level of imagery and comic exaggeration. Pensive reasoning, unobstructed by strings of images, however, builds on a stock of motifs and symbols familiar from his preceding works. As they are constantly varied, contrasted, and seen in a different light, the poems nevertheless acquire a calmer rhythm compared to the hectic rhythm of many earlier poems. Under Both Eyes signals a perspective of heightened awareness by its title and reiterrates it in the section "Double-Poems" through instructions to the reader. Andersen presents a series of double poems, that is, two poems on the same subject, but with a different thematic emphasis, for instance, "Old Man in Light" as opposed to "Old Man in Shadow" or "Nineteen-Year-Old Girl on Diving-Board" as opposed to "Nineteen-Year-Old Girl in the Air."

According to Andersen's directions, these poems need to be read simultaneously, "under both eyes" so-to-speak, to see the complexity of a theme. Such a procedure is similar to that of recalling the different view of a negative when looking at its developed picture. This technique falls in line with the camera perspective and special magnifying focus Andersen has been preoccupied with all along. As early as in Here on the Reserve it catches the reader's eye in the poem "Spell" ("Anfald"): "For a moment everything is suddenly reversed / the negative called forth / people's skin radiates with brightened friendliness / you are a big round eye yourself (...)." It is this kind of a spell that is taken up and expanded in Blanket-Toss, where it turns into an odyssey in space with a bird's-eye view at a disturbing twentieth century environment. Only "coming into the world"--being here and now, with both eyes, with confidence and love in face of life's complexities--amounts to the meaning Andersen emphasizes. Andersen's becoming more open as a poet coincides with the time when he and his wife Signe decided to separate in 1977. Under Both Eyes reflects a speaker who reasons intensively, who transmits the insight and the ethical position he has arrived at by taking the risk of expressing his message more directly to the reader or listener. This development in Andersen's poetry--encouraged by the personality of Cynthia Bramsen to whom Andersen got married in 1981--is also present in his first novel On the Bridge (På broen, 1981).

The recognition Benny Andersen has received as an author is based primarily on his poetry and prose works. While his popularity in Denmark resulted in record sales of his poetry volumes and of Svante's Songs, book and music alike, his works have not only appealed to the general public alone. The many awards Andersen already has received, as well as his election to the prestigious Danish Academy in 1972, attest to an equal acknowledgement on the part of other writers and literary critics. This broad acclaim of Andersen's work is due not only to the humorous portrayal of life's everyday difficulties that confront above all the "common man," but also to the critical psychological insight into human attitudes and inhibitions, which Andersen transmits through strategic experimentation with language.

Based on these general characteristics of his works, Andersen has been able to present a few major themes with an impressive variety of aspects. This study aims at demonstrating that the reason for such complexity in limitation lies in Andersen's preoccupation with essentially one motivating idea--authentic balance in life. That idea, essentially another approach to the theme of search for relative unity in a fragmented modern world, is the driving force behind Andersen's literary technique, one he uses to express dialectical patterns of thought.

Andersen's work certainly reflects the time it was written in, since it deals with problems and trends which we easily can identify as those belonging to our Western industrialized environment with its reverberations from world-wide political conflicts. But it also has to be kept in mind that its points of departure stem from the postwar period, when intense public debates linked ethical questions with the role of art, specifically with that of literature in society. Also Benny Andersen's works rest on a central question of ethics, with a focus on the individual. For this reason, his social criticism cannot be separated from his efforts to instill a sense of responsibility in his readers. The relationship between individual and society--certainly a prominently reactivated theme in postwar debates[28]--is explored in its dialectical processes by Andersen's close scrutiny of everyday life. His ethical program focuses on the individual personality and is clearly related to the concern for a responsible humanistic stance in life which Danish debates centered on during the early and mid 1950's.

Andersen names Søren Kierkegaard as one of his sources for inspiration,[29] and it is here, in his focus on the personality and in the dialectical pattern which extends to the tragicomic strategy in Andersen's work, that an affinity with Kierkegaard can be recognized. Furthermore, there is a discernable affinity in Andersen's work to the philosophy of Sartre, whose ideas spread in postwar Denmark with the reception of European philosophical and literary currents by Danish intellectuals. Dialectical traits in Andersen's poetry have already been alluded to by some literary critics;[30] this analysis of Andersen's poetry and prose will go further and concentrate on the underlying system from which his literary production derives its unity and impact.

2

Points of Departure: The Search for an Attitude Toward Life

In his first poetry collection, <u>The Musical Eel</u> (1960), Benny Andersen arranges his poems into four groups. These reflect stages in the search for an attitude toward life, positions which are formulated from the awareness of a personal state in flux without a metaphysical basis to fall back on. Most of the poems are written from the perspective of a first person speaker and represent points of orientation, as the speaker tries to come to grips with the realities of life, be they of the cyclical character observed in nature or of the seemingly trivial kind encountered in daily occurrences. There is a clearly discernible thematic development among the poems, and with regard to poetic technique it becomes evident that focus emerges as a pivotal concept, decisive both for the speaker's individual perception and for poetic depiction. The prevailing contrast between the ideal and reality, between expectations and actual confrontations is thus approached with the attitude that the ideal may frequently be a question of focus guided by specific humanistic values, above all the basic value of love. Thus the speaker's perspective is expanded beyond his limited view to include the world; his love for a woman breaks his isolation, and he thereby moves a step beyond the self-address so often found in Andersen's poetic monologues.

Along with the formulation of his ethical attitude--while never losing sight of the practical side of life--Andersen tends increasingly toward focusing on the fleeting moment as the poetic unit, thus freezing an unusual focus on ordinary daily events into

a momentarily magnified glimpse of the human condition.   Although
simultaneously a trend away from the first person to the more
detached third person perspective is discernible, the polarity
between the "I" and the collective "you"--between the individual
and society--remains as a challenge to the speaker and cannot be
resolved into a "we." Only the last group of poems containing four
prose texts marks a radical departure from the preceding poems.
Here, the return to the first person speaker culminates in a group
perspective of "we" with a passionate call for active individual
involvement. Each prose text, externally not distinguishable from
a narrative, fuses personal philosophy with social criticism into
a general program for the speaker. It amounts to a program of
personal commitment that can be considered binding for Andersen's
later works, no matter which literary genre he chose to express it
in.

I Nature and Society

Nature, indicated by the volume's title The Musical Eel,
serves as a major vehicle for the speaker to express his sudden
realizations and his philosophical reflections in the course of
his continuous process of discovery directed toward his environment and his own reactions. These poems are by no means simply
contemplative in character; they are constructed to rationalize
life's various difficulties as an orientation for living.   It is
not by accident that a poem like "Rural Station" ("Landstation")
opens this first collection, thus setting the tone for the entire
volume by introducing one of the most basic contrasts of our
modern experience: the meeting of civilization with nature's
unadulterated elementary forces.

> One March day you're sitting
> numb in a cold train.
> With a hyperdermic needle
> you are shot into the heart of Jutland.
>
> The train suddenly halts,
> tossing you out of yourself
> here where dark and
> light blood meet.
>
> Muddied fields
> with blots of snow
> keep a despondent eye
> on heaven's white doors
>
> like small boys
> who haven't eaten
> all their porridge and are afraid
> of their mother.

A constellation of wild geese
streaks across the heavens.
Is it my name that in their harsh,
mocking and distorted way they fling down?

Hesitating, as if to investigate
how much you still dare see,
a cow loose from her tether comes
toward you through the mud.
Silently gives birth to a calf in the snow.

You turn back, dizzy,
lose your way in this strange land.
Forget path and errand.
Notice only how the thick earth of Jutland
clutches your shiny shoes.[1]

Civilization is represented here by the city dweller in his "shiny shoes" who experiences his meeting with Jutland's interior as a disruption of his usual, balanced environment to the point of his feeling displaced, methodically and artificially "shot into the heart of Jutland" with planned hygienic accuracy. Quite unexpectedly he is tossed out of the habitual rhythm and into a strange, disquieting confrontation. The fact that witnessing a few basic manifestations of nature's laws causes him such confusion--shocks him into sensitivity--signifies not only that he lives his daily life away from and out of touch with nature's cycles, but his sensitivity also shows that he has preserved a potential awareness for phenomena which for the city dweller are rarely visible within the context of civilization. But in Jutland's rural interior, he is exposed at close range and alone to nature's unfamiliar dimensions. After the train has left him behind, there are few reminders of civilization, and the cyclical renewal of life after the winter months overwhelms the spectator by its immediacy: Fields emerging from under their wintery cover, slowly eating away the snow like children their porridge, the wild geese returning North unerringly guided by their sense of direction; and as if to prove the validity of their announcement of spring, a calf is born in the remaining snow before the unaccustomed city eyes of the poem's speaker. Because he is so unprepared for such a genuine manifestation of life unpackaged by civilization, Jutland's more rugged landscape and these common events in nature's course are in his view mapped out as a "strange land," where seasonal phenomena of nature impose a sense of the extraordinary on the beholder and make him feel small. They remain superior and resist his attempts to familiarize them by attributing human characteristics and motivations to them; they are not so easily conquered. Instead, both the wild geese and the cow appear to have conspired in captivating him by their uncomplicated coping with existence, thus reversing commonly assumed roles. They are perceived as being in control and fearless in contrast to the human spectator, slightly indulgent of him or even mocking him who is so unprepared for this natural autonomy and unable to balance elementary physical existence with civilization. His own

name seems to be flung down to him from "heaven's white doors:"
the overcast sky corresponds to the closed doors of heaven, which
are not eyed questioningly by the personified fields only, but by
the lonely speaker as well. The mockingly distorted cry of the
wild geese is heard against a background of silence.

Altogether, the events of an apparently harmless encounter
coalesce to become moments of existential awareness in which the
speaker loses his balance and his orientation as to "path and errand" and ends up dizzy, fleeing from the hold that "this strange
land" has taken of him, while the heavy soil is keeping a firm
grip around his polished city shoes. In contrast to nature, he is
not bound by the same regularity that constitutes its strength but
is alone with the choice of his individual path on an existential
level and not merely at an unfamiliar rural station. His dizziness points to the experience of existential imbalance when confronted with this freedom of choice.

Andersen conveys the breath-taking quality of this experience
by rhythmic correspondence. In spite of dividing the poem for-
mally into stanzas, he departs from conventional poetic form by
choosing a free rhythm without end rhyme and thus creates a rhythm
that corresponds primarily to the units of psychological perception. Rhythmically, the balanced meditation in the unit formed by
the third and fourth stanza intersects the brief choppy rhythm of
the poem's beginning two and last three stanzas, where an accelerated reception of events takes place. While rhythm achieves
such proximity to a highly subjective experience, the choice of
"you" singular instead of "I" creates a distance whereby the
speaker observes himself in his soliloquy, and at the same time
establishes a connection to his reader or listener. The speaker
as axis for this dialectical process of approximating and
distancing a significant experience is revealed only once in the
poem when he perceives the cry of the wild geese according to his
philosophical outlook: as a mocking of himself who is shut out,
alone with his doubtful approach to life--a weak approach compared
to the animals' sure pursuit of their prescribed paths.

"Rural Station" fits into a Danish tradition, in which the
vast rugged landscape of Jutland is depicted as providing a
disquieting experience of proximity with the forces of nature.
This experience is felt to be both awesome and unsettling, par-
ticularly for the Copenhagener who is accustomed to the closed
spaces of the big city as well as to Zealand's gentle landscape.
Kierkegaard reports such experiences in the journal from his trip
to Jutland in 1840,[2] and among Andersen's contemporaries, Ole
Wivel's account must be mentioned, because Andersen's poem "Rural
Station" bears a striking thematic and metaphorical resemblance to
Wivel's "Jutland Sonnet" ("Jysk sonet"). In these two poems,
Jutland serves as the catalyst for different reactions to the same
basic conflict of a lost religious belief. Like Andersen's poem,
Wivel's sonnet portrays a lonely wanderer in a rural setting, with
closed skies resting over a desolate marsh--an atmosphere of
deathlike silence that causes Wivel's wanderer to feel "the
universe / close in as fear and sunset's glow," while only gusts
of wind "murmur with ominous voices of madness / and are answered
angrily by the waves at the cape."[3] Although the doors of heaven

open to transmit a flood of gleaming light, the light is not perceived as the well known symbol of hope. Instead, a changed perception, stressing the accompanying shadows, suggests the wanderer's distance from the traditional symbol and the religious
belief it represents; the lines in which the light is addressed as
"late sunshine, heavy with ache and age--/ you oppress the heart
of an autumn-dreamer / with your shadows icy and dark" (105), also
indicate a nostalgic regret over having lost that belief. Such
nostalgia is absent in "Rural Station," a poem which almost can be
read as a response to Wivel's sonnet. Here the desolate landscape
and the forces of nature serve not only to reflect the speaker's
emotional state; it also creates an awareness of a human one-
dimensionality that has been self-inflicted and requires self-
help as implied by the speaker's impression that his name is flung
down mockingly from heaven by the wild geese passing overhead.

This poem's speaker is reminiscent of Nietzsche's lonely wanderer in the harsh prewinter setting of the poem "Vereinsamt"
("Isolated"), seemingly mocked at by the winter crows for having
shut himself out in the cold by cutting the ties which firmly an-
chor individual existence in a traditional metaphysical outlook.
Existential loneliness and isolation from the security of religion
dominate because traditional explanations no longer bridge the
persisting doubts.

As in Nietzsche's poetic soliloquy, it is necessary to face
and endure such loneliness, a thought which Andersen clearly expresses in "Just before Winter" ("Lige før vinter"). With a
minimum of a conventional abcb rhyme scheme, the three stanzas of
this poem assume a formulaic quality, as they convey the speaker's
reflections, self-admonishment, and encouragement since he needs
to make a vital decision concerning his attitude toward life.
Here, it is obvious that not Christian belief, but life itself,
the individual burden of existence, is given primary importance.
The risk of falling must be taken along with the necessary leap if
freedom and life are to be attained, if angst as a determinant
factor in life is to be overcome:

> Yours is the turned-away heaven.
> In darkness only, you can see what you want.
> Beyond the thought of salvation
> you will come to exist.[4]

The essential choice to live while accepting the absence of religious belief has to be made; darkness and winter take on a
liberating function, symbolizing an existential loneliness that
needs to be approached affirmatively in the quest for freedom from
implanted religious fears and promises.

Such acceptance of closed doors, of the turned-away heaven,
does not, however, eliminate continued questioning of the unknown.
In this regard, Andersen's "Novemberday" ("Novemberdag") constitutes a striking contrast to such a well known autumn poem of
the German literary tradition as Rilke's "Autumn" ("Herbst").
When Rilke observes the falling leaves, a falling to which we too
are subjected sooner or later, he also states reassuringly: "Und
doch ist Einer, welcher dieses Fallen / Unendlich sanft in seinen

Händen hält."[5] Andersen's "Novemberday," on the other hand, does
not express this faith in a secure falling:

> Naked branches are knitting in the wind.
> Leaves crumble like old letters
> the sun has read and burnt.
> The first snowflakes are falling
> into my warm hand and evaporate.
> Now, we sink down into space.
> Will we fall into living hands?[6]

Instead of a definite answer, only a question follows regarding
our function in the natural cycle.

It is characteristic of Andersen's work that, in spite of intense philosophical questioning, he never loses sight of the concrete social conditions he is bound by, as he laconically demonstrates in the conclusion to "Analysis" ("Analyse"):

> Last night I found my philosophy,
> and never have I slept so good.
> But where will I find an excuse
> for my having overslept?   (SP, 7)

To achieve a working balance in existence, is perceived as a constant challenge during our daily struggle of meeting our own ideal
expectations and those of others; adjustments have to be made constantly. Here, the comic with its distancing quality assumes a
key function, as in "Skeptical Prayer" ("Skeptisk bøn"):

> I pray for balance in life
> like the shopkeeper with his thumb on the scales:
> just let it look right!   (SP,19)

Be it taxes, atomic fallout, illness, or a difficult crossword
puzzle, the comic portrayal of the poem's speaker struggling with
an oversized burden of daily pressures all the way into his
leisure hours reveals a person who takes very seriously what he is
inundated by daily, although he appears to look only for a compromise; the poem, with its hectic rhythm, depicts a highly in-
secure person unable to relax.

Andersen, as indicated, observes nature closely. It functions not only as a catalyst for philosophical probing but also
provides orientation because of its many similarities to the human
condition on one hand and its cyclical regularity on the other.
The images are gradually losing their comparative character since
metaphors increasingly tend to replace similes. Nature is treated
as a personified universe in itself and provides a model society
for life's difficulties and constant coping; it teaches the
relativity of attitude needed to help balance the speaker's expectations of and thereby his attitude toward everyday reality. In
order to handle the slow progress made in fulfilling his expectations, the small creatures of nature are brought to mind in a
humorous adjustment of perspective, alluding to New Testament
phrases: "Blessed be the small ones of the world / that continued

to stay small, / the crawlers which continued to crawl / that time
we learned to walk."[7] Using the formulaic initial phrase from the
Beatitudes, the speaker reveals how the particular universe of the
small creatures serves as an orientation for his life: they assist
him in accepting his own slow progress by demonstrating that
achievements need to be measured by individual qualifications
rather than by imposed demands, and that "it is necessary to crawl
for the one who wants to learn how to walk."[8] This moral is later
applied in Andersen's literary strategy, in the sense that the
necessity of adjusting our perspective also becomes important for
the technique in some very short poems where the speaker's focus
personifies nature and often reverses commonly held views of what
kind of events are significant or insignificant. Accordingly, the
moving force in many poems is aimed at creating such awareness as
represented in "Widescreen:"

> I wander chilly and bloodforsaken
> and snap at the sunset.
> Widescreen! Hollywood! Technicolor!
> And glare down at the flagstones
> stamped with greasy leaves.
>
> Then a chestnut cracks at my feet.
> A bright brown eye opens.
> Beholds heaven and earth
> for the first time.   (SP,27)

This poem makes the reader aware that one small occurrence--the
cracking of a chestnut--may be just as spectacular as a monumental
sunset. When the focus suddenly switches from the poem's speaker
to the chestnut, human characteristics are bestowed on the chestnut, expressed in the metaphor "a bright brown eye." For one brief
moment, a vision is revealed in which the world is created at this
very instant, as if it were being seen for the first time. Rather
than taking on a consumer attitude and watching a pompous sunset
like a film in technicolor, the speaker singles out a simple
natural phenomenon--usually taken for granted--and, by way of a
biblical allusion, makes it extraordinary. That Andersen is not
fostering the idyllic nature poem should be obvious when we consider the implied metaphor of a widescreen technicolor movie for
the sunset. The speaker exhibits a critical attitude toward his
surroundings, including nature, and hints at our consumer habit of
being impressed by superlatives.[9] Furthermore, he sees the flag-
stones as being "stamped with greasy leaves;" he does not elevate
the banal into an idealized image. Such an attitude does not,
however, keep him from wonder, from admiring the small and often
overshadowed incident such as the opening of the chestnut.

The idea of creating a new perspective of our environment is
thematically present and taken one step further in the poem "Creation" ("Skabelsen"), where biblical creation serves as a model for
individual creation in all its complexity: the speaker sees himself and his surroundings come to life as his isolation recedes
through the experience of love.

In the third group of poems in The Musical Eel, Andersen excludes a first person speaker and concentrates fully on the brief
situation that opens momentarily like the camera's eye for ex-
posures of varying length. During such brief instants, the ambiguity of an ordinary situation becomes apparent and often transmits an uneasy or eerie feeling. "Bottle Skipper" ("Flaske
skipper") still maintains a distance from the uncanny by contrasting the secure harbor with the rough open sea beyond; out
there where the seagulls are fighting over a sensation in the
water, "the waves are wild and indifferent."[10] There is no place
for dreams; mere existence is at stake. But in choosing to stick
to the miniature ship secured in the empty bottle, the skipper, as
one critic rightly has pointed out, first of all needs to empty
this bottle[11] and thereby secures a dream that appears necessary
to cope with life. From the poems "Photographs" ("Foto-
grafierne"), "Headliner" ("Hovedsagen") and "Sleepless Hours in
the Summer House" ("Søvnløse timer i sommerhuset"), it is evident
that the security of civilization is an illusion. This illusion
can often be maintained because there is a qualitative difference
in the dangers of nature compared to those of civilization; the
latter are frequently more difficult to perceive, since our daily
lives seem securely regulated. Only in certain instants or sudden
occurrences does an uncanny dimension come to the surface, usually
by way of subtle tension or a fearful experience. Even when followed by a release of tension for the poem's central figure, the
severity of the situation is enlarged through the ironic,
tragicomic, or grotesque technique and culminates in a final
driving point.

"Photographs" thus stresses the extreme loneliness of the
elderly person.

> She stops and pauses for breath at the landing.
> All those stairs, all those years--
> Stands with the cold key in her hand
> and listens for thieves.
>
> Nonsense--there are only photographs in there,
> good-natured, prominent eyes.
> No one looks like that anymore.
>
> At last she glides through the slot
> like a thin letter to herself.   (SP,29)

The woman's momentary suspense in front of her apartment door,
listening for possible thieves, serves to emphasize her actual
isolation. It is not only a spatial but also temporal isolation,
as signified by the old family photographs, the only company she
can expect when coming home, friendly faces but of a past era.
The final point lights up this loneliness and hints at a lack of
communication with other people by playing with the double
reference of "slot;" it refers to the letter slot in her apartment
door as well as to the narrow slot to which she opens the door as
she enters, whereby she becomes a message for herself.

Andersen's interest in disrupting the routine perception of our surroundings by a suddenly introduced unusual focus is frequently accompanied by word play. In Danish, "Hovedsagen," meaning "the main thing," is compounded from "hoved" (head) and "sagen" matter or thing, and only used in its figurative meaning. When Andersen employs it in his poem by that title, he playfully draws on both the figurative meaning of the compound and the concrete meaning of each part. Although the pun cannot be translated literally, Alexander Taylor, in his translation, has arrived at an excellent solution to approximate the English version to the Danish original by choosing "Headliner" as an equivalent.

> Sirens--skull fracture--old woman
> who has nothing but money on her mind.
> The kids scramble up
> and catch the rolling coins under their heels,
> grownups become like children again,
> but the heirs shout by the deathbed:
> Is it true, Aunt Gunhild,
> there's not even a quarter left?
> And Auntie smiles wanly: Just think, children,
> my headache has completely disappeared.   (SP,25)

This is clearly one of Andersen's well constructed, lighter poems, and there may be disagreement among readers as to the subtlety of the pun but this should not lead to dismissing the poem as a clever yet too obvious word play. Rather, attention should be focused on the dimensions of the grotesque element introduced on the basis of the pun. Externally, the material plane is merged with the human plane through the idea that all of aunt Gunhild's headaches are gone when she suffers a skull fracture from an accident. At that moment, she physically loses her worries about money by concretely spilling it in the street. But behind the resulting surface distortion, which may still be perceived as being unpleasantly funny since it is phantastic in its juxtaposition, a very real distortion becomes visible: a merging of the material and human planes has also taken place in an ethical sense, showing that material aspects are dominating people's interpersonal relationships. A distortion of values is thus pointed out: "Grownups become like children again" as if they never had learned to make ethical distinctions; material concerns are overriding ethical considerations among bystanders and relatives who only display an interest in the spilled money. Andersen exposes their materialistic attitude and the prevalent lack of compassion. Although the central figure, Aunt Gunhild, is liberated from solely material concerns after the loss of her money, the impression of an inhuman situation lingers on because of the added irony that her relief occurs only on her death-bed. In addition, this relief contrasts with an apparently unchanged attitude among her upset heirs.

The theme of dehumanization is also present in "Sleepless Hours in the Summer House." It is evoked through the motif of life's hectic course in modern society, a concern which Andersen consistently expresses throughout his work. In this poem, he

dramatizes the inability to relax in a summer cottage due to pressure from obligations and threatening world events. When finally
"the dream's rotary press hums," it speeds up the sleeper's sense
of a lack of control over the frightening, inscrutable course of
life, a process that culminates in the vision of his own obituary
going to press "unreadable because of misprints." (SP,31) At the
same time, as the daily stress finds its outlet in this symbolic
nightmare, the alienation from such a life is also expressed,
since the announcement is meaningless to its reader.

In general, literary critics agree that Andersen developed
his originality in depictions of brief situations which provide
unusually perceptive glimpses of our environment. Some of them,
reflecting the tradition of the fable, became especially prominent
in this first volume. The society of nature in Andersen's fables
is populated exclusively with small animals. It is a microcosm
where the often harsh reality governing existence suddenly
breaches an idyllic surface or punctures a widely accepted and
persistently held ideal. The theme of reality contrasting with
the ideal is formulated in the poem "The Musical Eel," from which
the volume derived its title.

> Ashes flick off the sun.
> Awesomely the eyes of the snail circle:
> what distances!

> The duck lands on the lake
> noisy as a needle
> dropped on a scratched record.

> The eel leaves the lake forever.
> Looks back several times furiously.   (SP,33)

The sun's glowing red ball is effectively evoked metaphorically by
equating it indirectly with a burning cigarette, which can also
suddenly emerge from behind greyness when its ashes are flicked
off. Equally sudden is the duck's disruption of this awe-
inspiring and calm scene--most likely that of the setting red sun
in a calm evening atmosphere. The duck, unconcerned with
aesthetic considerations, disturbs the peaceful idyllic setting.
The duck is preoccupied with the basic task of arriving,
presumably after having spotted a feeding place by the water's
edge from where the snail's perspective had followed the sun's appearance. In depicting how such mundane behavior violates the
musical eel's aesthetic sensitivity, Benny Andersen symbolizes the
aesthete's conflict with basic facts of reality that make it difficult for him to co-exist with other ways of life around him.
Unable to balance an ideal view with what constitutes necessity
for others, the eel does not merely leave the lake in fury over
the offensive dissonance caused by the duck's landing; rather, he
is seen escaping from reality.

That reality not only contrasts with but also overrides
aesthetic considerations is a theme most succinctly expressed in
"The Critical Frog" ("Den kritiske frø").

The duck arranges his reflection
neatly around himself for the evening.
At last the right sensitivity
to the reed-warbler's glowing tones.
People stand still and listen on the path,
enabling the mosquitos to hit home
while the water rat discreetly
removes the noisy ducklings.

Only a small young frog conceals his ecstasy
behind a belch.   (SP,35)

The idyllic atmosphere at the time of the reed-warbler's evening
concert over the lake's peaceful surface proves to be captivating
in a double sense: for both the audience and the victims. Andersen creates an apparently harmonious tableau where the enchanted
passers-by may be confirming their ideal expectations of nature's
aesthetic qualities, unaware of the harsh reality in the thicket
of the reeds. The profits of this concert obviously go to the
mosquitoes and to the water rat, creatures which display only interest in procuring the means for their existence.   Consequently,
the critical frog's dissonant belch in this overtly harmonious
concert amounts to a reflection of the grave battle for existence
among the species from which the idyl detracts. One-sided attention cannot be afforded in such an environment. The concert motif
unifies all thematic aspects of the poem by hinting at the per-
former, his audience, and those profiting from it, even to the
point of incorporating the water rat as usher who by way of his
understated activity seems to contribute his services to the performance by "discreetly" ushering "the noisy ducklings" out of the
scene forever. In this case, the former poem's "musical eel"
would certainly not have to leave the lake in anger.
    In transfering human behavior and motivations to small crea-
tures, Andersen stresses the analogies that go farther than the
easily acceptable, pleasant similarities observed on the surface.
Here, the lake, or the duck-pond environment, with its am-
bivalence, becomes the focal point. It is reminiscent of well
known examples from Danish literature where it also served as a
setting analogous to human society, as in Hans Christian Andersen's tale of the Ugly Duckling or somewhat varied in Henrik Pon-
toppidan's   story   The Flight of the Eagle.   Benny   Andersen,
however, remains more general in the brief epic situations of his
poems; that is, he avoids a strong emotional effect centered on
one character and instead employs comic relief after having
depicted various, usually hidden aspects of daily challenges.
What appears as a humorous apercu serves to enlarge events already
a part of daily routine; in most cases, we pass them by, regarding
them as not being of immediate concern. In these poems, Andersen
focuses on the many neglected facets of life. As he lifts them
out of oblivion, he transforms them into vehicles for his concern
about the quality of life around us.   While gently nudging our
consciousness and sharpening our awareness for analogues that
function as a mirror, he employs his comic technique to prevent

the undue over-emphasis of the momentary enlargement of one facet. Just as Andersen increases the visibility of various aspects of daily coping--be it with imminent danger, the attitudes of others or, much more importantly, our own attitude--he in turn uses his comic strategy to cope with the realization of the multitudinous challenges of life. Both humor and nature thus take on a key function in Andersen's poetry, serving to approximate a concern and to consign it again to its relative position.

It is characteristic of this first volume of poetry that Andersen is conducting a search, groping for a personal stance, philosophically as well as poetically. In this process he scrutinizes his environment and finds that nature provides points of orientation because of its availability as a mirror for the ambiguity of life, for the constant process of balancing between the ideal and the actual situation. Nature in its complexity serves as a model for both observing and presenting individual and collective behavior patterns that can be viewed as being parables of human conduct. In a poem as early as "New Voices" ("Nye stemmer"), the last of the poems of the second group, this role of nature is clearly visible. In his search for a confirmation of his ideal, the speaker had come to the wintery duck-pond "to learn a richer language, to listen to unadulterated voices," and hears the ducks fly toward him "with voices like scissors clipping cardboard."[12] He concludes that "you must always have bread with you." This final point signals more than the speaker's witty but disillusioned acceptance of his observation that nothing is free. It also underlines that practical motivations cannot be separated from ideals. Accordingly, in deciding to begin with exactly these unrefined voices as he aims at a richer, more complex language, he acknowledges the importance of a realistic approach to life already stressed in the early poem "Analysis;" for his growing insight, these unrefined yet authentic voices constitute a beginning. The moral is similar to that of the poem "Crawlers" indicating the value of a start which, though slow, is nevertheless a beginning. Whereas the admiration of nature prevailed in the first two groups of this volume ("Rural Station;" "Widescreen"), that stance has visibly shifted in the third group. Here Andersen centers on human situations and scenes from nature with a parable-like dimension, yet he observes them from a distance, without including a first person speaker. It is not nature's cosmic superiority but a comparative detachment towards nature and civilization that governs the perspective in these later poems.

II The Formulation of an Ethical and Literary Program

In accordance with the development observed above, the volume's last group of poems marks a point of departure from the stance of the detached observer to a heightened awareness of the victim, the individual who perceives an acutely critical human situation in the context of a modern technological society. Externally, these poems differ radically from the previous ones, since they are composed as prose texts. Through a stream of consciousness technique, the first person speaker, while revealing as his model Rimbaud's stance of the poet as seer, expresses his deep concern about the crippling effects that his social environment has on the individual personality. This theme is varied in all four prose poems with an emphasis similar to Rimbaud's criticism of Western culture in "A Season in Hell;" they signal that at this point, on the structural as well as on the thematic level, the consequences of the search for orientation conducted in the preceding poems are about to be drawn. Each poem therefore contributes with a key motif to the formulation of an ethical and literary program.

"Hunger" ("Sult") opens this constellation, and once again two opposing forces are present: nature and civilization. But contrary to the situation in "Rural Station," it is now civilization which assumes the active role, with Nature as the sleeping addressee in this poetic soliloquy. In the wake of technological progress and of civilization's ruinous exploitation of human and natural resources, everything natural seems threatened. Flowers, reading leisurely, or the intangible, valued components of existence--moods and genuine feelings such as love, for example--are seen in imminent danger of extinction. The speaker's traumatic realization of this destructive process takes shape in a vivid stream of metaphorical language that adds up to a vision of despair spun off before us. It culminates in a poetic program which proves to be fundamental to Andersen's production and clearly reveals his turn to a stance as social critic.

In his vision of hunger, the speaker is cast in the role of an oceanlike junk yard for civilization's wreckless pursuits of a one-sided progress--with the added strain that his capacity is disproportionate to the amounts he has to stomach daily:

> I am just a puddle but constantly mountains are foundering in me, ocean steamers career and bury their noses in the mud at the bottom of my stomach. Solitary slack belches of oil disclose the place-- until everything has settled. Then the small rusty tip sticks out again, cannot be lulled to sleep, my secret hunger, my painful hunger![13]

The oily belches signify his oversatiation with the one-sided artificial diet with which he is being overwhelmed, and by the same token, they signify "a sunken code, a greasy bubbling SOS" signalling a basic dislike for satiation. Instead, it is that secret hunger he is craving to fulfill, a hunger that needs to be followed up by abstaining from the overwhelming diet which has buried the memory of genuine, natural signs of life. The speaker, with his distress signals, therefore appeals to personified nature, the assumed company in misery:

> (...)wake up, aren't you hurting too? I requested reading: let me go hungry for once, let me read

in bed: (...) Oh, each day, I forget something,
and where it was there is only hunger left.
(...)Just one day's consistent fasting, and one
would have made it! But radar soup, antenna
spaghettis, no, no room for flakes of moods. Wake
up and tell me: what is reading?
(61)

Because Nature, that "big body" with its "cosmic digestion," its
"holy intestinal tract" is perceived as continuously sleeping, the
speaker comes to realize how essential it is to rely on himself
and devise a strategy for dealing with an imminent crisis. Not
praying for help, neither renouncing nor demanding, are seen as
effective strategies; only one strategy counts: the speaker's al-
liance with one side of his own nature, his deepest hunger, a
hunger whose allegorical assistance results in creative action.
It is the speaker's only alternative to the disease of oversatiation that he contracted from civilization. While hunger has to
work its way out, the speaker needs to work himself back to his
inner self and to the core of his memory: they must meet in the
middle of all that is lacking, "all that does not satiate."(62)
The imperative voiced here clearly implies an ethical and literary
program for a new beginning to be accomplished through the creation of a more humane world from the memory: "Continents with
foaming coastlines and branches for the birds, caves for the
animals, light for the small and darkness for the lovers--from the
memory of that tired sour smell on a forgotten staircase." (63)

By emphasizing the importance of nature, simplicity, and
memory, Andersen shares the view of Hugo von Hofmannsthal and
Franz Kafka. In Hofmannsthal's "Conversation about Poems"
("Gespräch über Gedichte," 1903), for example, landscapes of the
soul--that is, remembered landscapes intimately connected with
emotional states that can evoke a wealth of feelings and
perspectives--emerge as a poetic ideal.[14] One of Hofmannsthal's
examples, "the smell of damp tiles in a hallway" (der Geruch
feuchter Steine in einer Hausflur"),[15] was quoted by Kafka in a
discussion he had with Max Brod in 1903 about their differing appreciation of contemporary literature.[16] It is the commitment to
unpretentious depiction of natural and fundamental, but often hidden or forgotten, dimensions of human existence that Andersen
shares with Hofmannsthal and Kafka, as visible in his programmatic
formulation at the end of "Hunger."

This program for creative action is directed against the
forced daily forgetting of treasured values--a process accomplished by the mechanisms of society which inundate the speaker
with "reeking traffic and pompous headlines, (...) coldy smiling
ammunition, whispering exam papers, the mercury of tariffs, the
tyranny of reserve parts;" (62) showered with such pressures, he
is involved with all his senses. Andersen treats this problem
with the call for a major defense action after the speaker's
awareness has reached a critical climax. Because hunger has come
to signify more than a vital lack, it actually points to a process
of reduction: the individual's freedom to forget by his own voli-
tion is gradually being eliminated through the pressure from ques-

tionable values. Memory therefore functions as a counterweight to restore this freedom by way of the creative process, that is, the SOS signals need to be followed up; the "sunken code" must be deciphered and the long forgotten reactivated, especially the memory of childhood with its proximity to unadulterated nature, to a time when life was still undisturbed by the rigorous possessiveness of civilization. Submitting to satiation would only result in values disappearing or becoming antiquated, in their being completely eclipsed by the pressures of daily routine and by the infiltration into the personal sphere of the ideal of progress, as interpreted by the media and a consumer economy. The defense strategy with which "Hunger" culminates, aims not only at creating but also at sustaining awareness of the necessity of change and the invitation "take me at my word" (62) thus functions as a challenge to the implied author of "Hunger" and to the implied reader as well. It remains to be seen, how this challenge is met in Andersen's poetic oeuvre.

The two prose poems that follow "Hunger," also deal with an individual reviewing his life at the moment of a drastic change of directions. "Possibilities" ("Muligheder") depicts a speaker who focuses on his adult life. Since he realizes how half-hearted it has been in comparison with his childhood and youth, he takes a radical turn. At this critical stage in his life, he can no longer ignore the fact that in his adult life routine took over and passion was levelled and replaced by phantasies about possibilities never achieved. He had been content with this escapism, indicated symbolically by his equating himself with the curator of his life's museum. Having reached a point near suffocation, however, he realizes that it is imperative for the survival of his individuality to assume an active role and make himself heard. "For who believes in moments, upright decisions, slammed doors, when everything can be reproduced, love in all phases, innocence utterly disappointing, spontaneity more genuine than the original."(64) In an age of reproduction of and thereby substitution for nearly every aspect of life, including feelings, the credibility of qualitative attributes such as genuine, unique, and natural has suffered; consequently, preserving them like a curator cares for the treasured values of his museum, has amounted to a futile strategy. What is required is not merely the speaker's faith in possible changes, promoted by his own phantasies, but passionate personal involvement and the courage to risk "a Fall." He realizes--as he needs to make use of his "right to scream"--that he has sold it by accepting the advantages of a comfortable, self-contained, but superficial life. The severity of the speaker's plight and self-accusation is indicated by his allusions to the human ventures of the Old Testament: to the Fall, to Esau's betrayal of his birthright, and finally to Noah's journey with the ark. Hoping to untangle himself from both the mediocrity of his environment and of his own stance, the speaker sees the need to become a passionate advocate of the genuine properties of life that seem to be disappearing. The possible substitutions conjured up earlier by his imagination must be drowned symbolically in preparation for a new beginning:

I shall let the impossible in here for a great
flood so there won't be a dry spot to see, not a
leaf from the olive tree for the dove to fetch.
The ridiculous I shall take seriously that which
is out of the question, I'll accept: mercy and
wonder, the dew and the sea, truth which cleanses,
silence which moves. If only I were worthy.   I
wish I were completely impossible!
(65)

This new start is of immense importance for the speaker's identity.   If he wants to survive as the promising person of his
childhood and youth, he has to choose and break out of certain
norms.   For society declares as unimportant, ridiculous, or impossible for the most part those humane qualities which he feels
are lacking, yet would help to counteract the increasing artificiality in our social environment.   While the program expressed in "Possibilities" corresponds to that of the previous
poem, it nevertheless goes a step farther in alluding to a poetic
technique that can be observed throughout Andersen's work. "The
ridiculous I shall take seriously" constitutes a key to his comic
strategy in both poetry, short prose, and dramatic works.
    In the poem "To One who Is Greater than His Disappointment"
("Til en der er større end sin skuffelse"), the motif of losing
face is symbolically depicted as unmasking and is explored in con-
junction with a serious criticism of society; for the mask--
synonymous with the mold administered by society--is torn off as a
new self-assessment begins for the speaker, only to leave him with
"bloody flesh" where his real face should have emerged.   This
state symbolizes a partial loss of identity and the challenge to
restore this loss. Motifs, familiar from the preceding poems,
reappear, among them the link with childhood via memory and dream.
The initial shedding of the mask presents the speaker with the
challenge of unifying his personality, a task he must face alone.
The other self, the missing, uncompromising part, has to be
retrieved from the labyrinth of childhood where it securely encapsuled itself to protect itself from an imposing world.
    To live without the mask, that is to admit our incompleteness
while aspiring to find ourselves and restore our credibility,
presents a major difficulty: how can we conduct a meaningful
search when we are constantly being confronted with misguiding
illusions that only lead to our superficial functioning?
Society's consumer goods readily provide prefabricated solutions
as substitutes for salvation and happiness, such as "the department stores where Ariadne thread is available in all colors, lawns
where four-leafed clovers stick out with annoying regularity."
(66) Social myths for daily living have been manufactured for the
consumer who, instead of looking for the authentic value lets himself be persuaded by the quality of the reproduction. Such a
"false nature"--as the French critic Roland Barthes termed it--[17]
constitutes a barrier in the search for genuine human qualities as
part of a well balanced personality; for the poem's speaker, it
ultimately poses the threat of petrifaction. To identify with
these social myths and prefabricated values which are symbolized

by the mask would lead to eventual stagnation; to live with these facial traits requires consciousness of their substitute nature. The speaker knows that a smile with these traits betrays itself in taxing situations: when trying to gain children's confidence or when pepping up a tired friend because they are not yet or no longer fooled by such substitutes but look past them for the original human values.

Since society, by way of a normative process of consumption, prescribes certain concepts of happiness and salvation, and assigns a specific consumable value to them, it influences people's behavior and the concept of their own identity. To escape from this molding process and from the imposition of such false facial traits appears to be impossible. In this predicament, only the knowledge of the other self's proximity lends the necessary support in maintaining the individual moral integrity for a fair assessment of this critical situation. Accordingly, the speaker not merely voices criticism of his social environment, he is also able to face reality in regard to his own involvement and concludes the poem by unmasking the role of the individual: "the environment, that's us!"(66) Although this poem does not join the others in proclaiming a specific program, it demonstrates through its perceptive uncovering of social mechanisms and the individual's position within this context a view of personal responsibility that must precede any meaningful action. The two-faced quality of existence has to be realized, the fact that the individual is both victim and participant, is object but also subject, and therefore can contribute either to affirmation or change of the existing social pattern. This existential situation needs to be realized and accepted.

With the last poem, "Escapism" ("Eskapisme"), a comprehensive summing up takes place, no longer from the perspective of a solitary speaker but from that of a first person plural speaker, thereby conveying the impression of a general concern about the decreasing quality of life. "Escapism" gives the most direct references to Western industrialized society of the mid-twentieth century. A grim environment is depicted here with its "forced urban planning, (...) blood clots, traffic clots, (...) children who are executed by cars if they play, grown-ups who just barely manage to let life pass, by daily taking a small advance against death in the form of pills, bottles, or books, even the flies are addicted to DDT." (67) The faith in progress, promoted for generations, has led up to this point where the damage of progress is felt to outweigh the benefits. It leads to a panic-like imperative, which resumes the motif of petrifaction alluded to in the poem before: "dissociate, escape to the plains, to the plains," away from the big city, and away from our hearts of stone, "the most vulnerable of everything."(67) That the problem is far from being solved by an escape from dehumanization--be it through a hardening of emotions or through a straight-forward escape--ought to be obvious. Consequently, the poem leaves no doubt about the ambiguity of the protest. As much as our instinct of self-preservation makes us aware of daily and long-range threats to life and environment, it also may cause us to choose the wrong strategy for self-preservation. To protest against the development of continuous dehumanization and the threat of extinction constitutes a beginning which must not merely end in escapism. Rather, we need to guard ourselves against letting our need for security dominate to the extent that it makes us decide on isolating ourselves in an encapsuled state symbolized by a "peacefully rotting hedgehog." (67) Long-range security is uncovered as being a myth and above all a dangerous one when it is self-centered, as the interspersed parable indicates: "'I am precious!' the pearl hummed. 'Then I am rich!' the mussel whispered and closed up."(68) The positive value attached to the striving for security--whether in the context of progress or in a protesting dissociation from it--only distorts the critical situation and covers up the necessary imperative. It is the present stage of development as well as our mistaken strategies that have become our undeniable responsibility. The poem therefore leads the motif of escapism to a climax by posing the question: "Is it possible to escape from escapism? (...) How can we survive all the vaccinations and life insurances?" The answer which follows opens a new perspective of the ethical program for action observed in the earlier prose poems: "By absorbing the shocks from far-away detonations through our feet and letting them unfold as caresses and open eyes." (68)

The challenge posed by the decreasing quality of life has to be met with a strong commitment to personal involvement in society's developments, no doubt an idealistic program. How it is to be implemented in our rushed daily reality--one primarily governed by pragmatic interests--presents itself as an equally challenging problem; although it is just barely implied in this poem, it amounts to an ethical imperative of caring and reaching out. At the end of his first collection of poetry, Andersen has reached a stage where a subjective and a collective point of view are correlated with a focus on an existential situation in a specific sociohistorical context. Even though he is mainly concerned with universal values, he still addresses certain specific concerns within the context of our modern, highly industrialized society--concerns, some of which were to be formulated with intensified protest by environmentalists about ten to fifteen years later.

The Musical Eel represents not only the foundation for Andersen's subsequent themes and techniques but, more precisely, also for his ethical attitude toward life. With its concluding four prose poems, this first collection culminates in a program for action for the poet Benny Andersen, who stresses that possibilities must not be reserved for the imagination and the distant future. Instead, they must focus on and "comport with"--to use Sartre's phrasing--[18] his passionate, active involvement in the reality of his particular sociohistorical context.

3

Social Identity

In the poems written in the nineteen years after
The Musical Eel, Andersen continues to address the complex problem
of existential security, carrying forward the themes developed in
this first collection, but with a particular emphasis on the
search for balance in life--the challenge which the individual
must accept after the fundamental experience of openness evoked in
"Rural Station." The overwhelming encounter with vast spaciousness
signifies a confrontation with life's boundless ambiguity and immense uncertainty, and a recognition of the absence of fixed
demarcations or definitive directions, be they of a metaphysical
or ideological nature. At the same time, society provides a
network of directives and strategies to live by--"omens" as Sartre
would term them--[1] that tend to prevent individuals from truly
finding themselves and from genuinely discovering meaning in their
lives. The frustrated heroes Andersen portrays in his poems are
therefore seen caught in the constant struggle of trying to meet
individual as well as social demands.
The ambiguity they confront derives from basic human concerns: on the one hand, they must realize and accept that, for
the individual perception, life has labyrinthine qualities and
constitutes--in spite of scientific progress--a temporal and spatial enigma, while on the other hand, they need to cope with the
specific conditions of life in a modern industrialized society.
Since the latter poses the more immediate demands, it is in this
daily twentieth-century existence--"Here on the Reserve," as Andersen terms it in the title of his 1971 volume--that the main
focus of the struggle lies. It is a cultural environment which

time and again throughout Andersen's literary production appears
strikingly hostile toward genuine personal growth and toward the
furthering of humane qualities in people. In The Musical Eel,
long before environmentalists and "concerned citizens groups"
began to campaign against the acutely increasing dehumanization of
our environment, the poem "Escapism" sketched a vision of or-
ganized death disguised as an advanced, highly cultured civilization. This kind of apprehension continues to form part of the
background for the close-ups from the social environment Andersen
perceives and projects in his subsequent poetry.

I Confronting Social Directives

In the modern individual's experience the environment seems
to be governed by an anonymous power manifested in relentless
daily pressures to perform according to certain set norms. In
every sphere of life--at work, sexually, in conversations, at
parties--the individual encounters the pressure to meet specific
expectations that reflect values based on superficial performance
criteria. Andersen brings these most emphatically to our attention in a number of poems whose dialectical structure consists of
a string of imperatives, a series of commands which ultimately
reveal the discrepancy between the requirements of society and the
demands of personal ethics, as in "Be popular" ("Bliv populær"),
"Be somebody" ("Bliv til noget"), "Keep on course" ("Hold kur-
sen"), "Keep your mask" ("Hold masken"), "Stop" ("Hold op"), "Endure" ("Hold ud")."[2] The individual's need to strike a balance
between integration into the established social system and commitment to the development of a personal identity constitutes the
dialectical challenge which unites these poems from Andersen's
volume Camera with Kitchen Privileges (1962). With good reason,
the Danish critic Poul Borum wrote that with this collection of
poetry, Andersen had found "both himself and us."[3] In their
straightforward recitation of an overwhelming mass of social imperatives, the poems signal the amount of pressure the individual
is conditioned by, and implicitly raise questions as to how integration can be achieved without compromising oneself, without
loss of meaning for oneself. The critical point of view disclosed
in these poems serves to direct protest against superimposed
values, that is, against a violation of genuine values which no
longer are deemed worthwhile because they are void of pragmatic
success criteria.

"Be popular" leaves no doubt about the basic premise that
must be followed if the individual is to emerge as a person from
social processes: "you must find yourself / or else others
will."(41) The ironic enumeration of society's directives which
follows this warning reveals a utilitarian, inhuman system
designed to mold people into a norm and prevent them from finding
their own identity. This social machinery fosters a frighteningly
high degree of mechanical behavior along with an attitude oriented
toward affirming the established value system. The insistence on

normative behavior tends also to suppress any criticism which
raises questions about the validity of the prescribed norms.   In
both private and public life, such a social machinery continues to
promote the pressures of the everyday routine at the   expense   of
humane interaction among people.   Under the pretext of helping individuals find their identity and place in society, conformity and
integration are fostered by means of norms for appearance and
behavior when communicating with others.   The resulting one-
dimensional value system exercises its power because it is disguised as a model for normality and thus reinforced by public ap-
proval.   "Be popular" illustrates that such conformity on the part
of the individual is necessary for personal success.

> (...)
> Keep an eye on buttons
> they say a lot about people's personality
> follow eyes that keep right
> hair that is lying down
> reward all those with coats
> talk to all those without saxophones
> try to understand
> (...)
> subscribe to ready-mixed debates
> organize conferences from many parts of the world
> direct them
> convene
> delegate
> compose
> do
> (...)
> they will like it
> topics:
> "Life."
> "Ibsen's line spacings."
> "Should the label be attached to the beer bottle's
>   back?"
> (...)
> But try to understand
> they will like it.
>
>
> And keep away from green violins
> blue thighs and indefinable chestnuts
> dissociate from the party's participants
> from those who sit in the dark
> don't listen to those who stumble over their words
> dismiss dreams with spelling errors
> exclude every kind of accident
> condemn the revolving mustache
> and the painting that needs to be fed every day
> fear those who cut off their buttons
> out of pity for their coats
> don't learn from those whose shouts boom
> through the soul's fall-out shafts

> utter dislike of used gauze bandages and St. Vitus'
>   dance
> boycott arms and legs that aren't attached to the body
> don't try to understand
> you won't like it.   (41-43)

The road to popularity, general recognition, and therefore to a place in society and meaning in life is clearly delineated; at the same time, it is uncovered ironically as a trade-in for potential authentic individuality. What "they" will like is the individual's involvement in a conservative machinery which is aimed at perpetuating itself, even if that means trivia will be emphasized rather than concerns of genuine importance for humanity. Ready-made opinions for debates and harmony through uniform looks, dress, and interests contrast sharply with everything and everyone that resists such levelling. The expressionistic images indicate how deviations from prescribed normality "green violins" and "blue thighs" are considered dangerous, how insecurity, unpragmatic attitudes, compassion, agony, and pain are viewed as obstacles by a firmly established majority. Consequently, those who are unable to secure their lives in a prefabricated balance expose the system's flaws by their very existence. Although the poem culminates with the imperative to repress the existence and the criticism of persisting problems, the ambiguity of the conclusion--"You won't like it"--suggests where society's vulnerability lies. After all, the likelihood that popularity may be rejected under such circumstances because of the intolerable inhumanity and utilitarian values cannot be ruled out and remains a dangerous variable in the system of social directives.

Precisely this variable can be regarded as the potential basis for a synthesis and as the actual focus for both the theme and the structure of the poem. Overtly, society's directives are placed at the center of attention, but their ironic escalation results in a shocking overexposure whereby critical questions arise about the quality of life, thus necessitating a synthesis. Not only does each poem in this group create such an impression, but the last poem, "Endure," also incorporates a turn toward open opposition in the interest of change. The ethical imperative not to ignore those whose position is antithetical to the directives of the social machine is expressed at least implicitly in each of these poems through the ironic juxtaposition of harshly contrasting attitudes.

Society utilizes the individual person's inner urge to find meaning and through it security in life; it propagates norms that seem to guarantee what is sought, as, for example, by way of distinction in "Be somebody"; since "there are always donors for plaster on stand-by," the individual can fulfill the distinctly felt obligation to train for becoming a monument according to the recommendation: "switch over to pedestals / then death won't be so bad." (44) Distinction that outlasts the transiency of life seems to promise personal fulfillment. But the inherent contradiction has been hinted at already, since such monuments are made of plaster and furthermore rest on specific pedestals-- certain names, papers, and lucky slips of the tongue--which sym-

bolize how superficial and often accidental their alleged guarantee is. Instead of meaning, these monuments denote petrification
and the implicit sense of the poem is that it is therefore man-
datory to abandon them. Any decision not to perform in accordance
with prescribed values, however, presents a threat to society's
version of harmony, while also exposing those who resist walking
"in the direction assigned" to a new set of obstacles. The theme
of levelling--the fact that "all music" is being "concentrated in
one scale"--receives further support from other symbols and from
the parody of the Ten Commandments in "Keep on Course:"

>keep right of opposing melodies
>thou shalt love the Lord your string
>there is only one string
>thou shalt not have other strings
>he who plays on several strings
>is lost.   (45)

Here, musical harmony achieved through reduction symbolizes confinement in a conservative affirmation that rules out any protest
and sanctions only one melody as acceptable. Of similar symbolic
quality are buttons, a recurring symbol for resistance, as opposed
to zippers, which are used to signify smooth adjustment, and
thereby the affirmation of integration and hence of confinement.
The only guarantee resulting from the acceptance of such
directives appears to be--momentarily at least--society's success
in perpetuating its system, even exporting it to underdeveloped
countries; "o-lands"--over-developed countries--constitute "the
adventure of our times" (46), a rather miraculous adventure that
consists of exporting an entire cultural pattern, including its
critical weaknesses. By pointing to the consequences of such ex-
ports, the poem "Keep your Mask" leaves no doubt about their ex-
ploitive nature: "your shadow must be cared for" (46)--you must
preserve you mask, the shadowy side of your personality. More
precisely, subscribing to society's one-dimensional norms equals
promoting our shadow, that is, our opportunistic tendencies.
Under these circumstances, self-preservation becomes a vicious
circle because saving face corresponds to holding on to a mask;
society's directives are revealed as being governed by commercial
principles, so that adhering to them means following the rules of
a basically competitive system: "live up to your mask / create a
market for it" (47). While the mask symbolizes the repression of
genuine values and individuality as already encountered in
The Musical Eel , it also suggests both the danger to the individual of permanent self-mutilation and the threat to the system
implicit in the recognition of this danger. Opposing the mask are
those voices in dark hollow spaces, in shafts, cracks and crevices
of conscience, familiar from "Be popular" where they were the out-
siders at society's festivities. Although still in the dark, they
are nevertheless recognized as an explosive challenge to the individual consciousness, even behind the protective facade of the
mask. The poem raises the question of how long the mask can function effectively as a repressive defense mechanism, how long a
profitable attitude toward life can be marketed without drawing

criticism from the system's own ranks, and in raising the question, alludes to a potential turning point.
　　These poems reflect the point of view of an individual
harassed partly by imperatives and perhaps self-persuasion, and
partly by a haunting awareness of human degradation.   They
strongly suggest that the system as it stands is untenable and
that it warrants an ethical stance of protest from the individual.
　　A more specific address is directed to the author in society.
In "Stop," the theme of integration by way of reduction emerges as
a twofold problem for the author, since it also affects the medium
of language.   A powerful yet endangered tool, language, although
it can create awareness, can at the same time be abused to
manipulate the interpretation of messages, for instance, by
reducing the complexity of meaning. "Stop" focuses on just such
an obstructed language, one which has been subjected to a one-
dimensional norm that assigns only one acceptable value to
words--"synonyms lynched by exclamation marks" (48). Although
"Stop" protests against irresponsibility of participating in the
blocking of messages by reductive use of punctuation and syntax,
the alternative, "a new generation of homeless idioms" doomed to
be "fugitives or interned / in giant parentheses," appears to lead
only to a dead-end imperative: "Never bring unfortified words into the world." Insecurity and the persecution of words and the
values they represent are, however, precisely the risks to be
taken if the underlying ethical imperative to restore the
repressed dimensions of meaning and of life is to be followed. An
ethical fortification, such as this one not only can but must be
given to the poet's words.[4]
　　In the spirit of this implicit commitment, the last poem of
this group, "Endure," calls directly for action and culminates by
accepting the consequences of the previous poems' massive antithetical construct; integration and its symbols of compromise
are rejected.

> It is irresponsible to keep quiet in a furiously
> 　　boiling world
> where flute after flute becomes silent
> impossible to live with ingrown eyelids
> and a Santa Claus-beard in your ears
> to retract everything again
> until speech consists of swallowing motions
> receipt on tomorrow's frontpage
> (...)
> what counts is not to be able to afford
> to be stingy with your death
> forbid the screen version of your death rattle
> refuse investment in your consent
> it is irresponsible to keep quiet
> at an exhibition of deafenings
> to hum along with your own death hymn
> no matter how obvious it is
> spit out
> even if stains should get on existence
> get rid of the tasty poison that paralyses your tongue

        do the forbidden
        speak with your own voice
        your first word
        good-bye paradise.   (49-50)

The continuous thematic escalation observed throughout this group
of poems is here channelled into satirical imagery whereby the
earlier motifs are resumed.   Individual consciousness of the
dangers of conformity has reached a critical point: even buttons
are being integrated, utilized to give "suitable counter-pressure"
and the "illusion of resistance" (49).   An intensifed sense of imminent danger is recognized and exposed as originating in an accepted norm of harmony.   Critical awareness is traded in for a
smooth way of life.   The result is a caricature of the individual
who has been reduced to a mere object vested with marketable
skills and attitudes.   In exchange for a kind of harmony whose
loudness has to cover up the absence of complexity, people consent
to a life with reduced vision, hearing, and speech, and swallow
the myth that such a life equals paradise.   This type of escapism
by way of integration is countered with a call for active
disengagement, for rejection of such social conditioning.   A conscious individual stance reverses the assigned moral labels of harmony, purity, and conformity: dissonance, spots, and resistance--
the voices from shafts and crevices--are rehabilitated as essential parts of existence.   The poem clearly indicates the necessity
to oppose any one-dimensional directives for integration and to
endure in the existing antithetical tension by means of self-
assertion.   Such self-assertion in favor of unpragmatic but
authentic human values is openly called for by the ethical imperatives "spit out," and "speak with your own voice," and begin to
follow your own directives with a "good-bye paradise."
     That the ethical commitment expressed here concerns both the
individual's and, specifically, the author's stance is strongly
reiterated in "The Stammering" ("Den stammende"), where escape into individual isolation is emphatically ruled out.   Instead,
metaphoric language becomes a key strategy for depicting the ur-
gency of a responsible and self-preserving reaction to a controlled environment.   Thus in the poem's development of the theme
of reduction, flags function as ideological blindfolds against
which the senses revolt.   In his soliloquy, the speaker formulates
the agony he experiences when attempts are made to considerately
bandage his eyes: "(...) your eyes are burning holes into those
flags" (56).   Whether environment is controlled ideologically or
with pesticides, violation of the natural requires active and
responsible resistance.   For the individual, the threat of an untenable situation is complemented by the threat of personally
sinking into oblivion if the challenge to speak out against
society's problems is ignored:

> if you cannot speak one day
> and moved by your own words are led away
> from your net of detested conduits and ways out
> to an unknown and stony locality
> from where you will supply us
> with unsprayed idioms.   (56)

Monuments are clearly rejected in the search for a meaningful life, recognition, and self-respect. The inner torment and panic that result from participation in a civilization with diminished genuine values call for a negation of conditioning, a rejection of blissful ignorance, comfortable though such ignorance may be, and for a protesting stance expressed in unadulterated language. The latter means especially a refusal of the type of indoctrinating language common to large circulation newspapers, whose contribution to social conditioning is significant.   The poem "Young" ("Ung") focuses on the theme of conditioning primarily from the retrospective point of view of the angry youth.   In the poems above, the imperatives were potentially directed to both the reader and, in the soliloquies, the poem's speaker.   "Young" operates also with two levels of address but at the same time with two different speakers, an outside observer and the observed person himself.

> (...)
> youth is pressed between clock dials
> spread out to dry
> on an absorbent sheet
> (certain kinds of newspapers are superior)
> that way one can keep all through life
> without really growing or wilting.
> He has graduated from the treatment.
> He spits and goes all the way into his pain
> goes all the way forward
> and looks out of his clear rage:
> I don't believe in this existence.
> Emotional life regulated with thermostats
> sublimated stomach ulcers
> the logic of roofing-tile whose conclusion
> is the drainage pipe.
> I am quitting as a hanger.
> (...)   (55)

Distanced, impersonal, in the style of a proven recipe, the seemingly detached stance of the observing speaker is betrayed by the sudden switch to a passionate outcry from the perspective of the recipe's object, the youth.   All the more vehemently, the reader is confronted with the theme of human reduction through social conditioning, through a kind of "treatment" which is criticized as a merciless molding process.   The repression of natural development, which results in stunted growth, is seen to have affected both feelings and reason. Society's agents in this process are clearly identified: schools where normative values are enforced and, as well, those large circulation newspapers,

poor in quality but rich in capitalized sensations. With his
angry refusal to continue such integration--to submit to what ultimately would be ossification in a prescribed social pattern--the
speaker's sharpened awareness gives a bleak projection of his surroundings: "everywhere the same landscape / the same houses the
same people the same scream," altogether the same uniform environment, including fear and pain.   The fact that "no one knows who
screamed / no one has heard it" is symptomatic of how effectively
conformity has dulled people's senses, causing them to react
merely with astonishment.   At the same time, however,   the
speaker's questioning awareness can cause their gestures and attitudes of astonishment to falter and in Andersen's strikingly
concise metaphor, come off their tracks.   The fact that their
former insensitivity can give way to an effort to reach out indicates hope for the ethical imperative the speaker has posed to
himself: "but I must find that scream / to make existence more
credible." This imperative reveals itself as essential for finding
a genuine meaning in life and as a commitment to unbalance
society's pseudo-balance along with its various sustaining symbols.
     One such symbol is dealt with extensively in   "Smile"
("Smil"), a poem which provides a string of satirical glimpses of
society and alludes to the molding of personality.

> I was born with a howl
> squalling I received my baptism
> yelled when I was thrashed
> shrieked when bees stung me
> but gradually became more Danish
> learned to smile at the world
> at the photographer
>   at doctors
>   policemen and perverts
> became a citizen in the land of the smile
> smiles keep the flies away and the mind clean
> and light and air are good for the teeth
> if you arrive too late
> if you go bankrupt
> if you're run over
> just smile
> tourists stream in
> to see smiling trafficvictims
> the chuckling homeless
> the cackling bereaved.
>
>
> I can't get rid of my smile
> sometimes I want to cry
> or just stand openmouthed
> or protest against other smiles
> that conceal bloodthirstiness and putrefaction
> but my own smile is in the way
> sticks out like a cowcatcher
> tearing hats and glasses off people

> with a smile I bear my smile
>   my halfmoon yoke
> where one hangs his worries out to dry
> I have to duck my head to the side
> to get through a door
> I am a citizen in the land of the smile
> it's not a bit funny.[5]

Contrasted with incidents which do not deserve a smile is the ideal of the smile in the face of adverse conditions. The speaker's identification of himself as "a citizen in the land of the smile," as a result of gradual conditioning, is an ambiguous statement, since the Danish term for citizen, "borger," also alludes to a middle-class attitude; thus the subsequent exaggerated examples of the smile at work can be read as a satire of a bourgeois standard. Using the diction of proverbs, Andersen distorts the content, so that proverbial guidance comes to bear a close resemblance to advertising slogans: "smiles keep the flies away and the mind clean / and light and air are good for the teeth." The request to smile, superimposed on exaggerated adverse circumstances, portrays Danish society as a grotesquely smiling advertisement for tourism. Ridicule is not kept beneath the surface here but brings the poem to an openly dissonant ending in its first half, wherein the smile symbolizes harmony as promoted by society; it is the artificially uniform melody from the poem "Keep on Course" that here can be marketed as a model to tourists. From the afflicted individual's point of view, the metaphoric depiction in the poem's second half emphasizes how thorough such conditioning proves to be even in moments of awareness and protest. The smile has become an oppressing burden, a "halfmoon yoke," superimposed on the individual personality, an obstruction whose proportions require grotesque depiction to match the speaker's feeling of powerlessness. There is no doubt about the totality of integration resulting from this molding process. Even if the smile has been distorted into an insincere grimace, this yoke also functions to integrate dismay and protest about itself. The abused smile, a dangerous weapon, threatens more than hats and glasses but also prevents self-assertion, is itself borne with a smile.

What Andersen shows, with his ironic directives and emphatic imagery, is how a profit-oriented society rests on superficial values and thus supports the dehumanization of its citizens. "Dreams with spelling errors," according to society's norms, have to be brushed aside in order to sustain the system, since they represent obstructions to smoothly running social dynamics. The individual person is therefore seen as caught in the situation, reduced to a functional level that is characterized and defined by a myopic view of values. This perspective elevates clichés to the status of values--for instance clichés of popularity and distinction--abandoning any measure of worth other than the strictly utilitarian. Consequently, these values confirm the existing superficiality, integrate it, and apparently succeed in justifying the established pragmatic norms at the expense of humanitarian concerns. The fact remains, however, that this system's ambiguity, like that of life, cannot be eliminated and is thrust into view at the point when the apparently well functioning superficiality begins to threaten those who subscribe to it. In keeping with Andersen's symbols, we might call it a question of zippers and buttons, or rather of the imperfection of buttons versus the smooth functioning of zippers. The loss of a button rarely causes a break-down whereas a broken zipper threatens the entire system it keeps together. It is these critical situations which Andersen, in another aspect of his social criticism, often focuses on in order to unmask the social myths people have accepted as guidelines, thinking that, by functioning smoothly, they are exercising control over their lives. Andersen exposes the system's shortcomings and our compromising stance toward it as well, continuously stressing--as he did in The Musical Eel--that "the environment, that's us."

II Coping Strategies

It becomes obvious in Andersen's poems that we are not merely the objects of an impenetrable system but actually contribute, consciously or not, to its perpetuation. The poems create an awareness of the dialectical process we must become part of. If the pitfalls of self-delusion and stagnation are to be avoided, integration into a false paradise must be as much resisted as the sterile confrontation of an antithetical deadlock. Such a deadlock, Andersen points out, may arise from the individual's choice of a coping strategy. Control over the pressure of daily demands is sought in a balance that needs to be achieved in life while facing the anonymity of the driving force behind these pressures. Such a balance constitutes a recurring theme in Andersen's work, perhaps most outspoken in The Musical Eel's "Skeptical Prayer," but also present subsequently in many subtle variants. The speakers in Andersen's poems attempt to gain balance by counterweighting the anonymity with concrete short-range goals or with the substitution of a dream or a prayer, skeptical as it may be. The guiding concepts in this endeavor are those of happiness and security; if they are realized, salvation from the surrounding pressures and the disquieting sensation that something vital is lacking in life seems to be achieved. This myth of salvation is central to the many strategies devised by Andersen's various heroes as they try to secure their balance in life. According to widely accepted and promoted social norms, happiness and security are to be sought and expected from various types of distinction such as popularity, recognition, distinctive looks, or an influential position in society. The underprivileged person's social dream, as depicted in "In the Bar," exemplifies this attitude which compensates for lack of meaning by adherence to a social myth.

Here gather small men with great voices
children of unwanted parents

around an overpopulated piano,
dreaming of handles, thick letters,
pregnant telephones
a life capped with foam.
Why live in a camera
with kitchen privileges
papered with null and void lottery stubs
cold showers for a hobby
and when sleep's plaster is ripped off
you find the day's abyss beneath you.
(...)
Here it is possible to believe
that the frame causes the picture
that all is good if only
we put the right words in the mouth of the echo.
We spin safe grooves
on intoxication's tranquil spiral
until the street outside is only
a little scratch in our dream's LP-record.   (SP,89)

Those who have experienced nothing but disappointment in their attempts to be successful and who consistently find themselves sur-
rounded by "null and void lottery stubs" nevertheless adhere to
the social model provided for their hope of relief from their
present deprived existence. The concentration on the lack of
material values replaces the concern about the lack of meaning in
such a dreary existence of repetitious disappointments.   It is
therefore not surprising when the strategy of seeking temporary
balance by means of alcohol and of escape into a gradually
mounting euphoria induced by the melodies of the piano player at
the bar only leads to another kind of consumerism: here, frustration is integrated for the sake of momentary relief into an illusion until identification with the model has been achieved in a
state of intoxication. A prefabricated dream has been bought and
consumed under the pressure of social conditions.   Combined with
the individual pressure engendered by the failure to succeed, it
becomes a burden which is periodically integrated into the rhythmic cycle of drinking, sleeping, lottery play. Andersen's technique of playing with fixed idioms is here visible in his exchange
of the common expression "an unwanted child" to "unwanted
parents;" it bears with it the sudden switch from an accepted to a
largely ignored perspective and underscores these small men's
basic dissatisfaction with their lot.
     As much as the poem concentrates on the existential situa-
tion, it has to be kept in mind that it is above all focused on a
socio-historical situation whose key metaphor, "camera with kitchen privileges"--the title for an entire volume with a large
number of outspokenly critical poems--calls forth an image of a
boxed-in, restricted existence. The added concession, access to
the kitchen, only makes the absence of privileges more painfully
obvious, and thus the confinement in a living-space from which the
so-called better life--the wealthier, more distinguished life of
the upper class--is perceived through a small opening. But the
important aspect of the metaphor lies in the fact that the projec-

tion received through that opening is registered upside-down. The poem's question: why live in such a camera? can therefore be formulated: why live under conditions that are not merely poor but are clearly perceived as wrong? Possibly, they can be exposed as being wrong as Karl Marx has done with a similar metaphor equating such living conditions with the reversed picture inside a "camera obscura."[6] Or they can be integrated, processed, and transmitted by adhering to the appearance of the model, a common reaction among "small men," as the French critic Roland Barthes points out in his analysis of social myths.[7] Compromising by accepting the belief "that the frame causes the picture" amounts to an uncritical submission to those values which sustain the perceived contrast in living conditions. The flaw in the existence depicted in Andersen's poem results from the choice of these "small men" to stifle their own awareness of faults in the system; instead, they accept the system's coping strategies.

A great number of Andersen's poems center on the exposure of such attitudes and strategies, usually through an ironic portrayal of types, including deviants, who do not live a full life because they have settled in a role. Their compromises benefit neither themselves nor others even though they may appear to do so temporarily, as through the chosen isolation in "Autonomous" ("Uafhængig"), "Sponger" ("Nasseprins"), "Man of World" ("Verdensmand"), "The nice Man" ("Den pæne mand"); or through dominating others with their attitude in "The Intellectual" ("Den intellektuelle"), "The Moralist" ("Moralisten"), "Beau" ("Galan").[8] The difficulties encountered by the individual are given an added dimension when a clear deviation from social norms takes place, for then we are able to see how, in a hardened antithetical situation, society's own coping with opposition competes with the individual's coping. Especially in those cases when the individual conscience resists integration into society's mainstream, the risk of being publicly ostracized is high, as Andersen shows in "The Hanged Informer" ("Den hængte stikker").[9] Here, society's self-righteousness is exposed because it distorts historical facts and assigns the role of informer to cover up for its own faults.

In these poems, society is always active in preserving its glittering self-portrait, bent on removing any obstacle in its way, be it "The Homosexual" ("Den homosexuelle")--"the solitary stubble on a glistening clean-shaven chin"[10] -- or the social critic in "Difficult Case" ("Vanskeligt tilfælde").[11] For such deviance only "the merciful shaver and saviour" or amputation of free speech are given as alternatives and a most uncanny perspective is opened on how far society's suppressive mechanisms can go. Society's strategy for brushing aside obstacles consists first and foremost in creating myths and shaping public opinion about them preferably at an early formative stage in peoples' lives. Above all, the myth of a social paradise with guaranteed security, happiness, and salvation--if social directives are observed-- dominates life "here on the reserve" and it is this myth which is constantly revealed as false in Andersen's poems, either through the exposure of its inherent contradictions or, at times, through an individual's open protest, as in "Young." The fact that values are distorted is reflected in these poems by the technique of grotesque distortion, so powerfully employed in "Smile" and "Headliner."[12] Andersen's criticism of a facade of smiles may well be unacceptable to those who view the poem merely as an enumeration of distortions of a positive value, and the later poem, "Difficult Case," might even cause a defensive reaction because of its seemingly far-fetched comparison of the Danish with the Soviet state.

In "Difficult Case" Andersen does not use distorted images; instead, he directly attacks society's treatment of people who differ from the majority and its norms because they attempt to follow the directive of their conscience. Ironical ambiguity is kept to a minimum, nothing obstructs the strategy of direct social criticism. The speaker here, unlike those in most of Andersen's poems, represents a group, "we;"[13] concerning the group's location, we are informed that "we" are "here on the reserve" with a constellation of group versus isolated individual. Rendered in the style of a medical bulletin, the poem leaves no doubt about the group's affiliation. The individual is characterized as a patient by the speaker, who--in a tone of regret--describes a deeply troubled, rather mixed-up person: "Water in the heart / blood in the head," a person preoccupied with "freedom of speech persecution tolerance." The patient, however, is not to be identified as an advocate for a specific political faction; rather, we receive the impression of a person still searching, fluctuating, of someone who is not jumping onto any faction's bandwagon: "right pulse oriented toward the left / and vice versa / blood pressure quite liberial / but conscience raised highly." In that state, he differs from society at large and is considered abnormal by the group's spokesperson: "there is not much hope / beyond the patient's own." The statement's irony lies in the fact that the patient's hope for an acknowledgment of human values such as freedom of speech and tolerance is not merely shrugged off as self-deluding but actually proves to be exactly that. He falls victim to a gigantic apparatus oriented toward self-preservation and strongly supported by experts who are traditionally considered to be ethically untainted and solely dedicated to the service of humanity. By contrast with the patient, they are revealed as deeply in trouble because they have confused humanity with the system. Consequently, their service is aimed at helping the social system survive. The patient therefore has to be integrated into society's system in a way acceptable to the supporters of the system: "If we take action / it will have to be amputation / of an estimated part of the psyche / litigation of certain speech abilities / so he instead of 'freedom of speech' / 'persecution' and 'tolerance' can manage with / 'fr-fr' 'pe-pe' and 'to-to' / thus he saves energy / and can possibly make it."

Under the pretense of help, the recommended surgery amounts to a plan for silencing the patient and eliminating social criticism in order to guarantee society's continued unisono. Benny Andersen has the euphemistically described procedure culminate with a satirical point: "we don't dare promise anything / but do a little more than we can / we send no one to Siberia / here on the reserve." Like in so many poems, Andersen plays with an everyday idiom, "we don't dare promise anything but do what we can,"

changing it slightly, we "do a little more than we can" to   reveal
satirically the discrepancy between limited competence and an announced intention to disregard those limitations.   In   the   poem's
context,   this idiomatic distortion--humorous if it were placed in
a harmless context--lends powerful support on the linguistic level
to the exposure of distorted values and intentions.   The speakers
obviously are both misusing their skills and abusing human rights.
Having led up to the concluding statement by means of an enumera-
tive approach, Andersen gives it the   quality   of   a   punch   line,
touching off the complex topic of the treatment of dissenters in
the Soviet Union and other countries.   At the same time, he is im-
plying through the statement's hypocrisy that we don't need to
send anyone to Siberia because we are creating our own Siberia
"here on the reserve." The poem thus shocks the reader into awareness with an alarming example of how society copes and enforces
the balance of its system against dissenters.

      This   and   many   other   poems   from   the   1971   volume
Here on the Reserve mirror Andersen's critical awareness of social
processes at the time of student unrest, anti-Vietnam-war demon-
strations, and the War Crimes Tribunal.   His active involvement as
a writer is more directly reflected in the anti-war poem he contributed   to   the   Vietnam-anthology Ord om Vietnam   (Words
about Vietnam), published as a joint venture by the three major
Scandinavian publishing houses in 1967.   In his parabolic prose
poem "The Warriors" ("Kæmperne"), Andersen shows precisely the
same distorted utilitarian values and strategies employed for
gaining control, but this time in the setting of the Vietnamese
controversy, where the peasant, the true citizen of his country,
falls victim to his so-called protectors, the foreign warriors.
The contributors to the anthology, an international group including outspoken authors like Wolf Biermann, Erich Fried, Robert
Bly, Lawrence Ferlinghetti, Göran Sonnevi, protest vehemently
against the war and against the inhuman self-righteousness
displayed by eminent figures and their supporters in Western
states and churches.

      The general focus of Andersen's social criticism, however,
lies primarily on Danish society, although it extends readily to a
large segment of Western culture.   It should also be stressed that
Andersen never practices a one-sided form of criticism.   Instead,
his efforts are consistently aimed at pointing out the dialectical
nature of social processes, true to his proclamation from
The Musical Eel that we constitute the environment.   He therefore
uncovers not only society's inherent contradictions and hypocrisy
but also the irresponsibility of individuals who integrate themselves and "daily with a smile dust the rim of the precipice."[14]
In Here on the Reserve, his stance as observer exposes how "almost
professionally self-effacing" it is to submit to society's myths
and directives.   Contrary to its stated goal of ensuring safety,
security, happiness for the individual, the pressure to perform
and conform results in "nailbiting for life." From the distant observer's   viewpoint   at   the   beginning   and   end   of
Here on the Reserve, submission to such a way of life equals "a
preferred type of suicide." According to this "Conservation
Report" ("fredningsrapport"), people have   reached   the   stage of

being an endangered species whose strangely contradictory behavior is motivated by the best of intentions, the wish to protect and promote life.   Quality of life, encompassing natural and social environments in our culutre, thus is scrutinized closely in Andersen's poetry in the interest of genuine human values and of achieving a relative balance which does not amount to the mere compromise of a pseudo-balance. Confronted with the challenge of living in this kind of environment, the individual cannot afford to ignore the discrepancies. The existing antithetical situation must be faced with courage if we are to depart from this apparent paradise.   It is the first step in arresting ossification and beginning to grow, an essential step in attempting to resolve the confrontation between social identity and personal identity. It initiates the ethical imperative in this dialectical pattern: "you must find yourself," better late than never!

4

Existential and Social Balance

Although society's pressures to follow fixed demarcations are
shown in Andersen's work to exercise a profound influence on
people, the poems also insist that the pressure of coming to terms
with the fundamental uncertainty of life cannot be ignored.
Anonymous but always present, uncertainty not only pervades the
everyday social world, as in "This Uncertainty" ("Denne
uvished"),[1] but also manifests itself in an entirely other dimension as in "Just to Be Sure" ("For en sikkerheds skyld") where the
speaker loses all confidence in the accuracy of measurements that
a yardstick can provide.[2] The latter poem's tone of desperation
points to the basic existential uncertainty which, in many of the
poems, is treated thematically by means of focus on individual
consciousness as it meets norms other than those provided by
society. When the fundamental categories of time and space reveal
their infinity in sudden moments, they serve to remind the individual that a more encompassing definition of balance in life
has to be achieved. Existential and social balance must complement each other if the challenge "you must find yourself" is to be
met realistically. For the individual, this implies the necessity
of defining a meaningful attitude toward life in general and
toward society in particular. It is this fundamental existential
disposition which Andersen expresses in a number of poems through
close-ups of the individual's perception of time and space.

I Freedom and Limitation

The experience of spatial openness is rendered variously in a series of poems in order to symbolize the alarming freedom that the individual must master. In "The Atlantic on an Empty Stomach" ("Atlanten på fastende hjerte"), attention is centered on this experience and on its sudden and powerful effects.[3] Symbolized by the ship, the speaker's journey on the sea of life is presented as an increasing yearning for open spaces and, simultaneously, as a distancing from fixed points such as a secure harbor. Complex yet small in relation to the ocean's vast space, the ship constitutes a link in the chain of the universe, seemingly autonomous: "a link which plays chain." The underlying dialectical process of balancing autonomy versus dependency, however, emerges at high sea as the speaker is confronted with the open ocean and senses the audacity of his venture. He has embarked with an affirmative attitude, but at the same time he acknowledges his vulnerability, his need for protection from such "incomprehensible greatness," for some way of keeping his glance from slipping while his eyes are "pecking seasick at the universe." Although modern technology provides the means for protection, allowing him to conquer this open space with a photolens and reduce its powerful impact to fixed dimensions of 24 x 36 mm, the immediate effect of this limitless freedom--this lack of stability all around--manifests itself in a sudden loss of balance. The mental agony of the individual who catches a glimpse of the totality of the universe is thus transposed into seasickness. It is not until he returns to the ship's interior, where the "quiet center of the storm coincides with the stomach" and where eventually the sink in the cabin is reached, that he is able to gain temporary relief and control. Having been thrown off balance at a moment when he was unprepared to be reminded of this boundless spatial and temporal superiority, he must now face the meaning of his own position and define his own function within this vast system. Like the ship, he represents only one minute individuality, "one millionth of a bridge / a fragment of comprehension;" with his limited autonomy, he is dependent on tangible dimensions for orientation on his life's journey. Inasmuch as the shift from the open Atlantic to the cabin sink provides a minor hold again in the practical world, it is also clear that no lasting relief is guaranteed. For individual consciousness, the fundamental challenge of balancing the cosmic and earthbound realities of life remains. Although the poem's title distances us from the philosophical by referring to the practical aspects of this experience, it also indicates that this existential challenge cannot be separated from the practical everyday.

A similar symbolic experience is known from Kierkegaard's journey to Jutland in 1840, when he lost his way in the Jutland heath:

> Alone on the burning heath, surrounded on all
> sides by sheer sameness except for the undulating
> sea straight ahead of me. I became positively

> seasick and desperate over not being able to get
> closer to the woods in spite of all my vigorous
> walking. (...) Simply because a person has such a
> wide vista out on the heath he has nothing at all
> to measure with; [4]

It is once again the overpowering dimensions of nature which serve
to emphasize the absence of a reliable measuring stick vis à vis
an immense range of vision; that is, they bring to awareness the
overwhelming freedom from definite guidelines for action. Both
Kierkegaard and Andersen transform the individual person's immediate feeling of human insufficiency and _angst_ into seasickness,
and for Andersen, such existential dizziness has become a frequently occurring theme since "Rural Station." It is often accompanied by the theme of support mechanisms, such as the 24x36 mm
photolens in "The Atlantic on an Empty Stomach" that organizes
spatial infinity into an illusion of definite borderlines and
stability. Andersen's symbolic depiction of this thematic complex
relies in many instances on the clever utilization of the spatial
category for his imagery. Read as a parable, "The Atlantic on an
Empty Stomach" signals that the stability secured from the fixed
borders of the photolens is not comparable to the actual experience but rather misleading later on when documented in the
shape of the finished photo. The validity of such stability for
individual balance is, therefore, as limited as when it is derived
from the knowledge of scientific laws, a validity which is
questioned, in a similar situation of nausea, by Roquentin, the
main character in Sartre's novel _Nausea_ (_La Nausée_). In both
cases it is dizziness or nausea that serve to emphasize the absence of secure barriers whenever nature--believed to be ordered
in fixed, abstract categories such as space in Andersen's poem--
suddenly makes its presence felt and overwhelms the individual. [5]

In the poem "High and Dry" ("På det tørre")--a scene from
personified nature--Andersen contrasts an attitude which seeks
limitation to one which willingly faces the unpredictable open
space with all its concealed dangers and mysteries. Limitation,
on the one hand so necessary to counterbalance cosmic infinity,
can on the other hand quite easily be turned into an idealized
crutch. This negative aspect is represented in "High and Dry" by
the kind of stability which excludes life's inherent ambiguities.
The lighthouse, a recurring symbol in Andersen's poetry, bears
witness to the self-deception involved in clinging to one
restricted outlook on life.

> The spruce saws away at the horizon
> while the dunes cautiously
> peep out behind one another's shoulders.
> Low tide. The scowling black stones
> rise up and lick their lips
> with tongues of seaweed.
>
> Pale and bitter, the lighthouse stares
> at the gloating jaws of the boats--
> What distant shores have they tasted--

What place could be more beautiful than this?

A dried up starfish
pointing in all directions.   (SP,67)

The lighthouse, firmly anchored in its spot, functions
traditionally as a symbol of safe guidance through hidden dangers;
it ensures a secure passage into the protection of a harbor, and
directs us in this poem to a beautifully ordered landscape at the
coastline. But at the same time, its position is contested by the
boats with their "gloating jaws," which represent a perspective as
open as the sea they are crossing. The risk they are taking in
their ventures to distant shores contrasts vividly with the defensive stance of the lighthouse, which, bitter about its contested
superiority, tries to hold on to its firm conviction that it oc-
cupies the best of all possible positions: securely "high and
dry." The validity of this view does not remain unchallenged; it
is emphatically opposed by "a dried up starfish" trapped on the
dry beach at low tide and, in a warning gesture, "pointing in all
directions." The narrowly viewed stability symbolized by the
lighthouse is supported by other images which reinforce the impression of stagnation we receive from the low tide and the dried
up starfish. The dunes' cautious hiding behind each other's
backs, when facing the open sea, accords with the provincial attitude of the lighthouse. We seem to be looking at a cross-
section of human types transferred into nature, as Steffen Hejlskov Larsen has pointed out in his analysis of the personification
used in this poem.[6] Whether it is the anxious caution of a conforming mass of dunes or whether it is scowling black stones
licking their lips with satisfaction, all seem to cling to the
conviction that no other place is more beautiful than this particular one in which they are rooted or have settled.
     Recognizing the ambiguity of life, even accepting it, may
sound like a simple enough task. But Andersen's poetry does not
cease to demonstrate how difficult it is to live up to the commitment to avoid stagnation. Maintaining a balance with respect to
spatial dimensions signifies a maintaining of growth, a resistance
to limitation or to becoming rigidly fixed in one position; but it
also signifies the necessity of knowing existing limitations well.
Concerning the individual's development, this challenge to obtain
a balanced, meaningful stance in life is dramatically formulated
in "This Is" ("Her er"), a poem of an intensely unified symbolic
structure which centers on the figure of the acrobat.[7] Although it
is not unusual to find the art of living expressed by the art of
audacious artistic balancing with a high risk of falling, this
poem's focus lies on how the speaker arrived at a point of no
return, where maximum balance is required. While he is at a loss
as to how he should continue, a possibility for balancing the individual and the social dimensions emerges.

          This is the large city where we live
          This is the narrow street in the large
             city where we live
          This is the old house in the narrow

           street in the large city where we live
This is you in the house
yes this is you
and this is me
in the middle of a sentence
in the middle of a TO that stretches in all directions
like a caterpillar at the end of a straw
This is the TO that turns about at the end of something
that isn't going any further at the moment
like a mast-acrobat I saw as a child
the mast was high and wobbled and swayed
eight meters to each side according to my father
I got a devil of a pain in my neck from looking
     so high
but got off really cheaply in comparison with the
     masterful daredevil
who later
or was it his predecessor
broke mast and neck
This is the neck which bears the head which
     remembers the neck
which sooner or later fell down from the swaying mast
and broke against the pavement of the street
     in the suburb
where I stretched my neck toward the presumptuous
and from this stems my later weakness for climbing
shipmasts powerpoles eventually streetlights
This is the pupated person
who came from the child beside the mast in the suburb
to the large city where we live
the swinging capital at the end of the road
which went through my clinging suburb
my neckaching childhood
my trialclimbing youth
This is the spine that leads up to the neck
which bears the head which uses the eyes
which saw the acrobat sway at the end of the mast
in the suburb that clings to the large overcrowded city
                              where we live
This is the head that sways at the top of the still
                                   erect spine
before your eyes
eight thoughts to each side
These are your eyes that are aimed at the TO
that I caught sight of at the end of the swaying mast
in the childhood I now have climbed up from
to the point where I can go no further
This is the TO
and this is you
yes this is you
Reach me a little finger.   (SP,75/77)

The street acrobat at the top of his swaying mast becomes an
analogous figure to the speaker, who has climbed up from childhood

through youth to adulthood and has reached a temporary impasse.
The moment of consciousness in which the sensation of facing a
void is experienced coincides with the sudden inability to state
the implications of having reached this point in life. As the
void opens in the middle of a sentence, the experience is linked
to two key symbols--the caterpillar and the mast-acrobat--each
denoting a different symbolic value. Although they appear to fulfill the same function at first glance, that of balancing in a
surrounding void, their functions are complementary rather than
identical. Both have in common the implied aspiration to
freedom--from a merely earthbound, weighted-down to an unencum-
bered existence; but owing to their given nature, they should be
seen as contrasts. While the caterpillar suggests a qualitative
stage, that is, the individual in the cycle of his development
having not yet reached the phase where he has freed himself into a
butterfly, the acrobat symbolizes an attitude which implies quan-
titative in addition to qualitative action. More precisely, it is
an attitude that requires that the individual repeatedly choose to
realize his freedom by gaining distance from the earthbound and
approximation to the freedom of flying. What this symbolic juxtaposition signifies is a truth basic to the human condition: the
individual cannot expect simply to develop to the stage of freedom
but has to make a persistent effort to reach the point where
freedom becomes a possibility. At the same time, the neck-risking
task of trying to achieve the relative amount of freedom possible
in life becomes a question of life and death. Failure to realize
one's individuality corresponds to spiritual death. Having
reached a stage in his growth, the speaker, accompanied by the
acrobat as ideal and model, recognizes that he is still a pupated
person; he has developed to this point and finds himself confronted with the void at a moment when he has to decide how to
realize his ideal and himself, and how this personal state of
isolation can be overcome. Even if the experience is a highly
personal one, the imperative at the end of the poem overcomes this
isolation by including the speaker's partner in the necessary action with a call for assistance, thereby expanding the concept of
individual balance to one of mutual balance based on the confidence found in friendship and love.

From a structural point of view, this poem's unity of images
has been developed in an exemplary fashion, drawing line by line
on all the biographically essential parallels for thematic support. Following the progressive development of the two key initial symbols, a gradual merging takes place, by the end of which
symbolic congruence between the speaker's person and the various
symbolic units has been achieved according to the following cor-
respondences:

straw	caterpillar	butterfly
mast	acrobat	artist
youth	pupated person	individuality
road	suburb / capitol	society
spine / neck	head / eyes	consciousness
sentence fragment	TO	request
I / me	you (sing.)	we

At the moment of conscious impasse formulated by the poem, the flashback to the swinging and swaying acrobat not only fuses past and present but also the symbolic figure with that of the speaker, his social context, and his efforts of communication. The theme of balancing thus captures an ethical conflict: the constant struggle for free self-fulfillment is a struggle to preserve erectness and to avoid slavish compromising of this ideal. Although this struggle by necessity centers on the individual, the large-scale implications cannot be overlooked. Individuality constitutes the first essential step; it needs to be further realized through communication and interpersonal relationship--not least for the poet--if a free, fulfilling, and balanced life is to be achieved in society at large. The ideal needs to be extended from the speaker to the "you in the house" to "the narrow street" to "the large overcrowded city," that is, ultimately to "the swinging capitol at the end of the road"--the society he lives in which has brought him this far. Accordingly, the speaker's monologue transcends itself in the concluding request for cooperation, just before the silent expectant partner assumes an active role. This request to reach a little finger may well be read as the continuation which bridges the void and follows "the TO" as the individual recognizes that a request to continue together is the only meaningful resolution. A balancing of the freedom of development with factual limitations--while avoiding the trap of inertia idealized as stability or security--clearly emerges here. The unbalancing existential experience already familiar from "Rural Station" and "The Atlantic on an Empty Stomach" is transcended by stepping out of individual isolation.

As the above examples have shown, Andersen defines the process of infinity as a balancing act that requires acknowledging human limitations but also allows the freedom of an open-minded self-development. This is also stressed in "Toddler" ("Tumling") through the speaker's statement that we must balance with the congenital weight around our foot thus describing the individual's situation parallel to Sartre's definition: "from the instant of my upsurge into being, I carry the weight of the world by myself alone without anything or any person being able to lighten it."[8] Andersen demonstrates commitment to balancing human limitations with human development through continuous personal efforts "to gain new dizziness."[9] Comparing the individual person to a toddler in view of spatial and temporal infinity, he focuses on the spatial dimension to symbolize the cumbersome exploration of a person's possibilities for development. Since the Danish title of the poem is not restricted to the meaning of toddler but, instead, covers three different meanings of English "tumbler," this range of meanings offered by the title alone sets the tone for the poem; be it a little toy figure with a weighted and rounded bottom, a toddler, or a certain breed of domestic pigeon, they all share as their natural approach to moving through life an uncommon mode of moving ahead. It might even be perceived as counteracting their forward motion. Stylistically, this struggle is vividly expressed through the contrastive use of the active and passive forms of Danish verbs. The forms of verbs as well as the rhomb-shaped typographical arrangement characterize the cumbersome, struggling

movements which symbolize a process that can be termed the process
of growing through life, an exploration of the surrounding living-
space in terms of the various modes of daily moves and encounters.
While acknowledging the constraints of natural limitations, here
represented by gravity, the individual person--only "seemingly
convinced" that such limitations constitute an end to
development--counteracts gravity by exploring possibilities of
moving on.

A number of poems in Andersen's works, among them such examples as "Astray" ("På afveje") and "Life" ("Livet"), support the
commitment outlined in "Toddler" by stressing how difficult it is
to live meaningfully in the absence of an unfailingly correct
direction and in the presence of "cemented agreement/ passable
traps," and "ways" which "are in the way," when "byways" may actually provide the meaningful direction sought by the individual
person.[10] It is the seemingly roundabout way that Andersen had
also underscored in "Life" when he wrote that it is above all important to "get absorbed in the start / devote yourself for hours
to your warmup run / with body and soul."[11] Andersen's poems thus
consistently project an affirmative attitude toward life which
insists--like the speaker in "To Summer" ("Til sommeren")--"that
human beings are indomitable."[12] Part of such a stance is an acceptance of life's duality, as, for instance, the coexistence of
absence and presence seen in "A Hole in the Earth" ("Et hul i
jorden"). The poem accentuates the interdependency of these two
qualitative states, contradicting the common perception, which
governs a more myopic view of life, that the two are mutually exclusive.

> A hole has come in the earth. Empty.
> Without earth around it
> it wouldn't be there at all.
> The hole is deeply dependent on the earth,
> an emptiness that shows something exists
> something that shows this emptiness exists.
> If the earth wasn't there
> there would be no emptiness either.
> From hole you have come
> to earth you shall return.
> Or vice versa.
> I warmly pat the hole
> and keep going on earth.   (SP,141)

This poem's speaker demonstratively shifts the emphasis away from
a one-sided perspective. Although the humorous play with the
biblical verse sums up concisely the little there is of certainty
in life, definitely birth and death, it also stresses what is
decisive for the relative balance possible: to realize the mutual
conditionality of emptiness--that is, absence--and presence. For
the fundamental questions of where we come from and where we go,
the interdependency of opposition is offered as the essential certainty. The hole, "a nothingness to be filled" symbolizes "a mode
of being," an affirmation of the individual's contribution to
"making a fullness of being exist in the world," in Sartre's

words; also death, which is usually regarded only as the subtrac-
tion of an individual life, is viewed in Andersen's poem as a contribution to the creation of a "fullness of being" as indicated by
the humorous word play--a dialectical view quite similar to the
one held by the influential Swedish poet Gunnar Ekelöf.[13] To go
on living affirmatively with the knowledge of existing emptiness,
requires remembering that it presupposes the presence of
something. Andersen expresses the necessity to, first, accept
these facts and, second, recall them periodically in another poem,
"Here where it isn't happening" ("Her hvor det ikke foregår"):
"Emptiness attracts fullness, / Some day life will / be known and
loved / if you don't desert your emptiness."[14] It is no doubt a
question of attitude and perspective, not least for the poet,
which--considering the similar stance expressed in Ekelöf's poem
"Poetik" ("Poetics")--again brings to mind the common basis of Existentialist ideas shared by Andersen and Ekelöf.[15] Maintaining a
receptive mind or--to use a frequent symbol for it--open eyes is
intimately linked with the challenge of balancing. The act of
seeing a positive and a negative side simultaneously, with both
eyes, as carried out in the "double-poems" of the 1978 collection
Under Both Eyes, is characteristic of Andersen's literary technique; moreover, it is indicative of the dialectical thought
process inherent in his work.

II   The Competition with Time

The experience of space is paralleled by the encounter with
time, more precisely, with the fugacity of time as it is experienced by the individual who recognizes that life is just "a
quivering fiber in death's muscle."[16] In a brief symbolic moment,
the finite and the infinite coalesce in a vision of death, when "a
matchstick flares in space / briefly lights up a face before it
dies." The scene evokes the sensation of surrounding spatial emptiness and of individual loneliness in space as darkness is
pierced momentarily by the appearance of a face. At the same
time, this manifestation of life in the vast darkness of space exemplifies how transitory life is. As it quickly fades away, we
can sense the presence of death, for the action parallels an x-ray
of life with death emerging to penetrate the consciousness of both
speaker and reader:

> Kiss right now
> before your kiss strikes a skull.
> Soon you will be no one
> but now you have lips
> and matches.   (SP, 133)

Through the focus on individual life as a point in space and a moment in time, that is, as a minute, transitory component of the
infinite, this poem underscores the relativity of individual existence and admonishes both speaker and reader to use the allotted

fraction of eternity consciously.   Whether the speaker is ad-
monishing himself or exhorting his readers, this reminder transcends the isolated personal experience not only by virtue of the
formulated address but also because of its implications for interpersonal communication, here symbolized by "lips and matches." In
other words, it amounts to an imperative with a distinct social
dimension: the invitation to reach out and interact meaningfully,
to spread warmth and love, is thus formulated as a personal necessity and responsibility as well.
     Such a realization of time's fugacity is essentially a know-
ledge which temporarily and intensely surges out of oblivion, carrying with it the double pressure of coping with the given factual
condition and of living up to the ethical imperative. This pressure exercised by time is explored in a number of Andersen's
poems, foremost in "Time" and "It's High Time."
     In Andersen's preception, time looms as an overpowering
phenomenon; in the poem "Time," its infinity is measured by twelve
clocks and is thus brought under the control of manageable dimensions, a strategy familiar from "The Atlantic on an Empty
Stomach," where spatial dimensions are tamed for human consciousness by a photolens. Once again, the poem depicts the individual
caught between the finite and the infinite, this time precisely
between the subjective perception and the objective progression of
time.

          We have twelve clocks in the house
          sill it strikes me there's not enough time
          You go out to the kitchen
          get chocolate milk for your spindly son
          but when you get back
          he has grown too old for chocolate milk
          demands beer girls revolution
          You have to make the most of your time while
               you have it
          (...)
          You would like to make the most of your time
          but all the time it stays away
          what becomes of it
          was it ever there at all
          have you used too much time
          in drawing time out
          You have to make the most of time in time
          roam around a time without time and place
          and when the time has come
          call home and hear
          "Are you calling 95 94 93 92?
          That number is no longer in service."
                         Click.   (SP, 129/131)

Although the speaker deals with a common daily problem and
distances himself from it through wordplay, he intensifies the
feeling of our powerlessness when confronting time to an extent
that borders on the absurd. The focus on detail so common to Andersen's poems is transcended here to confront the reader with a

compact view of life from the speaker's experience. Playing with idiomatic expressions, he carries us through hectic progression of time, as through a series of manipulations by some anonymous power. Moreover, feeling himself caught in the twofold perception of time, he projects us too into the apparent comedy, which actually amounts to the distorted image of a film being run too fast. Time in its measurable familiarity and its shocking anonymity is personified by the familiar and at the same time impersonal voice of the operator, which leaves the caller behind like an abandoned marionette, lost in time and also lost in his living space. It is the confrontation with absurdity combined with the hint of death that results in a sudden chilling effect. Surely it is easy for the reader to identify with the futile race for additional time; but that should not prevent us from realizing the critical potential expressed in this poem. After all, it reflects an attitude toward time which does not make sense because it superimposes our wishes on the factual situation.[17] We are constant competitors of time, even though we cannot reasonably afford to see ourselves as equals in such a disproportionate match. We are, in fact, transferring a behavior pattern from the social world to the category of time. Accustomed to progress in our twentieth-century environment, we are so used to trying to conquer the unreachable and control the untangible.

Andersen's play with idiomatic expressions signals another level of our response to the pressure of time, our felt obligation to utilize it effectively: make the most of it, draw it out, roam around in it freely. We need to achieve a sense of fulfillment in order to counterbalance time's fugacity. Thus, whether we attempt to measure time with a great number of clocks or try to create tangible lasting representations of good times such as photographs of exotic vacations in younger years, we are involved in an effort to gain control over our individual dependence on time. In this subjective relation each of us has to the process of time, it is imperative for us to find a special meaning for our existence.

This need manifests itself in the pressure we feel to achieve something in our lifetime, especially in view of a world filled with problems; it creates a tense atmosphere for living, as Andersen shows in the poem "It's High Time."

It's high time
the water boils
the earth burns
the world is waiting
when Alexander was Caesar's age
he was already The Great
when Caesar was my age
he had had it
they did not waste time
time did not waste them
they used time like a shirt
slept with it on
ate with it on
were buried in it
and here I sit

```
hold newspaper
hold Christmas
hold back
let exploits walk by my nose
(...)
the world does not wait
(...)                                         (SP,51)
```

A point of critical, if not catastrophic, dimensions has been
reached here, with the speaker experiencing both his own urgent
need for action and some sort of public expectation which requires
extraordinary involvement and effort of him. It is a moment of
sudden consciousness stemming from the fear that time may be
running out for achieving--privately and publicly--that special
recognition which seems so necessary for self-esteem and existential meaning. Here, a model is sought in the exceptional person's
relationship to time. It is perceived as a relationship of mutual
action: "they did not waste time / time did not waste them." In
resorting to such models in his attempt to respond to the pressures of time, the speaker signifies most clearly his adherence to
the social norm of efficiency and outstanding achievement. He
seems to be justified because he is fulfilling what he considers
to be his obligation in the face of public expectations: "the
world is waiting." This attempt to compete with time on the basis
of mere social pressure to perform reveals a distortion of values.
They have misled the speaker in his drive for existential meaning,
so he searches outside of his own personality and overlooks the
imperative to find himself. Others have already found him, but he
has not realized it, and so submits himself totally to social
pressures because, in fact, "the world does not wait." The world--
or society--is not interested in the individual as such but rather
in utilizing his endeavors for its own system.
    The sudden outcry "it is high time / it is past time"
therefore resembles an awakening, a recognition of the absence of
meaning in the everyday routine of the average citizen. But even
in embarking on the venture of fulfilling great expectations by
way of an unknown yet presumably meaningful action, the speaker
does not change the norms by which he lives. Consequently, the
discrepancy between his exalted sense of mission and his mundane
habits triggers a tragicomic effect: "my hat / my coat / my cy-
cleclips / it is now or never: (SP,53). The symbols of orderly
middle-class attire are carefully maintained in spite of the sensation of accelerated panic which propels the speaker through
shorter and shorter lines to the poem's end; they contrast vividly
with the high aspirations we can deduce from the previously given
models and serve to lend him a Don Quixote-like quality. In the
speaker's figure, the existential and the social aspects are thus
merged. His high aspirations correspond in their proportion to
the pressure he feels--the time pressure he feels not only because
of personal and public expectations, but also because of the size
of surrounding problems. The poem's composition, too, exposes
both, the excessive pressure and the incongruity of ideal and
reality, even down to the linguistic level. Here, Andersen
strings together idioms which allude to a banal everyday on the

one hand and to a worldwide perspective on the other: "the water
boils" is thus combined with "the earth burns" and places the
speaker's world, and ultimately his aspirations, into a dispropor-
tionately large context. The juxtaposition of "two conflicting
worlds" leads to ironic exposure of the speaker's behavior, as
Keld Zeruneith has pointed out.[18] Zeruneith criticizes Andersen's
use of irony from the point of view of the reader's reception; he
sees the poem as ending in a deadlock situation for a desperate,
yet ridiculed, speaker whom the reader looks down on with a
feeling of superiority.[19] But it is precisely the tragicomic effects which expose a misguided ideal and raise questions about the
norms the speaker conforms to. Even if exaggerated, they point to
the fact that he was taught the very discrepancy to which he ad-
heres, schoolbook ideals of heroism which pass over--and maybe
gloss over--the reality of his everyday life. The poem thus in-
vites the reader to look critically at the speaker's norms and
models.

Time thus receives representational value for insurmountable,
often anonymous pressures on the basis of its abstract or elusive
qualities. Sometimes complemented by the similar qualities of
space, time also serves to link the task of individual existential
balance with the determinants in society and the implications for
society. How subtly the categories of time and space are adapted
to a speaker's psychological state of mind and how closely they
rule his daily life is revealed in "Slug-a-bed" ("Syvsover").
Here, getting up in the morning becomes the symbol for the required integration into social pressures perceived through the
challenges of time and space. Thus for the speaker, getting out
of bed is a chore he resents.

> Immense impossible morning
> where you never get out of bed
> or even reach the edge of it
> so far flung it is
> large as a county
> you worm your way
> under the clammy lowhanging featherbed
> lonesome lost spermatozoon
> in no condition to get there
> (...)
> you are expected out there at the featherbed-frontier
> with questions, appointments, chutes, ties
> you're expected to awaken
> it's your duty to dig yourself out
> once a day
> and show up
> eat a little
> grow a little
> stand in line waiting your turn
> stretch
> bow
> sign something or dance
> make up your mind
> make your way

```
make do
but I'm all fagged out
because of all this featherbed
that pushes itself in front of me like a glacier
what is being transmitted through these feathers
send out a felt morse code
to toetapping authorities
tea rattling relatives
watchdog teachers and creditors
I am alive but enfeebled beforehand
start a search
with radar, frogmen, St. Bernards.          (SP,45-47)
```

Andersen offers more than a humorous look at a quite familiar situation in this sympathetic depiction of a person's concentrated efforts to leave the warmth and security of the bed as the time to get up inevitably approaches. He points out the extent to which we have become objects of our environment, how the duty to grow, show up, eat, and interact with others is felt to outweigh the joy of living. Joy, in fact, is never mentioned, only the obligation to live in a certain way.

Andersen uses the categories of time and space to illuminate the details of daily coping through a close-up view of one major aspect of it: the first action to be taken in a full day of varied confrontations. Spatial dimensions are adapted to the individual psychological state and acquire subjectively perceived proportions: the immense morning in a far-flung bed corresponds to the feeling of being overpowered by society's expectations which will take their usual demanding course from the moment the speaker has managed to get up. In the face of these already audible pressures—the sound of "tea rattling relatives" announces that time until breakfast is rapidly diminishing—the speaker's consciousness of himself shrinks to a pars pro toto perception: a "lonesome lost spermatozoon"[20] he worms his way toward meeting the well known array of demands. Once he has conquered the space up to "the featherbed-frontier," the pressure of time will take over, along with that of behavior patterns determined by social hierarchies. He is caught in a balancing process between trying to get up and not really wanting to get up; he views his initiative as wormlike, a micro-organism's endeavor compared to the overwhelming and compact pressures to which he feels himself subjected—particularly since the daily duties have begun to dominate his life. The mere thought of the extent of their influence, triggered by the morning sounds from the kitchen, creates a wave of panic that is proportionate in size to the request for rescue from his state of helplessness. Although the featherbed, insurmountable barrier and at the same time protective shield, illustrates the antithetical process through humorously disproportionate dimensions, no synthesis can be visualized except for the recognition that whatever needs to be done will require the help of others. It is the nature of such assistance, that the reader is left to speculate about.

The consciousness that our environment actually does not seem to serve us but that we instead seem to be subjected to its mechanisms, is heightened whenever a new beginning is necessary. Each morning, and especially each Monday, such a beginning--with new contacts and confrontations to come--has to be made, and each morning brings with it renewed awareness of the degree to which social pressures dominate all interaction among people.   Andersen pursues this theme in the poem "Monday" ("Mandag"), where the speaker's superiors represent to him the "big bad wolf" from "Little Red Ridinghood," taken over and multiplied to appear as father, teacher, boss.[21] Small aggressions and gestures of intolerance overshadow Monday, as everyone appears to be struggling to adjust to others again after the weekend pause. The same image as in "Slug-a-bed" is used and extended in "Monday," emphasizing the need for a change:

> But the way it is at the moment
> you cannot get out of bed
> are mistaken for your featherbed throughout
>   the day
> can hardly notice the difference yourself   (26)

Even though the speaker has managed to get up in this poem, he is identified as still having to deal with the same problem. The central image of the featherbed signifies self-protection and a barrier raised against other people, an inability to communicate by means of humane interaction. In contrast to such an attitude, the poem's speaker calls on us to direct our attention to discovering positive qualities in each other, thus eliminating the Monday- and the morning-blues.

Both the request for help and the call for a rejection of the hostile aspects of the everyday emphasize the fact that existential and social balance are interlocked. The existential angst experienced by the individual as he confronts the complexity of time and space is projected into the daily social world with its overpowering demands. It thereby becomes evident that facing uncertainty and powerlessness requires foremost a balancing of norms. Here and now, in the everyday environment, a meaningful self-development has to take place based on an acceptance of life's complexity and on genuine interaction among people.

III Orientation

Andersen brings to our awareness the dual quality of time, and the necessity of a commitment to use time here and now--not simply profitably but on a scale proportionate to the problems we confront daily. An expanded ethical imperative was alluded to in "Monday;" it could be read as: you must find yourself to make the world around you more humane and thus more meaningful. That such an effort is not a stage of development left behind in youth, is a theme directly addressed in the poem "For Orientation" ("Til orientering"). After many years of a successful, balanced life, the speaker is suddenly overpowered by the same intense longing

for a life filled with meaning and joy that he had experience as a
thirteen-year-old.   It is another example of the existential dizziness triggered by contact with nature which we meet throughout
Andersen's poetry. Here, the festive play of light and shadow of
an October moon brings together the two points in the speaker's
life through his experience of the same existential feeling of
longing, hope, and expectation. This moment of consciousness that
something vital is still missing in his life is "hard to accept"
for the successful adult.

> (...)
> and yet I felt at the sight of that
> moonwindowopening from which
> surged soundless golden music
> swinging the magnified shadows of the dancers
> dizzyingly around like a carousel
> the same thirteen-year-old helpless sigh for THE PARTY
> the party behind all cloudwalls and parties
> The Urparty
> life behind life!
> There I walked in the night, abandoning myself to
> An October moon and a cloud riddled with holes
> to something that wasn't in itself IT
> but reminded me of it
> was a reflection of it
> like the flag for the Nationalist
> like the panties of the beloved for the fetishist
> like the wafer and fruitwine for the Christian.
> And when the beam of light turned away from my path
> I felt abandoned
> drained in five minutes
> of the feelings of many weeks
> which could have been used for something
> real to make this world a moreworld.
> Indignant and shocked too
> at noticing the high tide of this feeling
> lifted by a dead planet.
> The object of the feeling was nothing in itself.
> But the feeling was true.[22]

The lack of this vital element--"life behind life," the meaning of
life--makes itself felt through the unbalancing sensation of
"longing toward a moreworld." No substitute such as those the
Nationalist, the fetishist, and the Christian have accepted as
meaning can satisfy this lack. Andersen's technique of grouping
three examples--his "triad principle"[23]--resumes a familiar motif.
Fixed demarcations--such orientations as ideology, sex,   or
metaphysics--constitute only a reflection of the meaning sought.
This hunger for the authentic is to be satisfied through a
"moreworld," but not in a romantic withdrawal from the world, as
his moonlight euphoria might lead us to assume. With a reference
to natural laws, the speaker counters any such supposition
beforehand by voicing his indignation at having been emotionally
at the mercy of "a dead planet." Nevertheless, he feels abandoned

and lost when the symbolic reflection of his belief in an existing
meaning fades away, taking with it the euphoria that could have
given him the energy to work toward this "moreworld," toward
reification of meaning in everyday life. Implicit in his experience is the persistence of existential loneliness, poignantly
revealed in the double meaning of the line "The object of the
feeling was nothing in itself;" "nothing" ("intet"), in Danish,
also refers to "nothingness," which after all is the object of the
speaker's feeling. How to deal with nothingness and with the absence of a tangible a priori meaning, "the Urparty," remains a
question at the poem's end. Speaking through other poems, we can
answer: by remembering that "nothing" presupposes "something,"
and by trying to work toward this "something" here and now without
abandoning this emptiness and this longing in favor of settling
down like a lighthouse. In other words, the speaker must fill
"nothingness," must create the meaning of his life and thereby a
"moreworld" in a continuous process regardless of material
success.[24]

In this thematic context, the need to keep on moving, to stay
aware and adjust the chosen course periodically, is an often
varied motif. Andersen by no means ignores reality in favor of an
ideal; he stresses how difficult it is to live up to this commitment under the daily load of duties. Thus, on "certain days /
when your clothes smell of shipwrecks and dungeons / even before
you creep into them,"[25] the speaker is confronted with the sudden
realization of how much has been neglected already. This realization of how much still needs to be done to meet just his own expectations threatens the apparently secure balance of his life.
As his soliloquy indicates, such a realization leaves you "with
just the skin on your nose and one and a half feet on the ground,"
and, above all, reminds that "you have to begin all over again
every time."[26] The art of living, then, consists in meeting the
challenge to live consciously, while acknowledging that, in the
complicated process of finding ourselves, society exerts an early
and powerful influence on us through its norms, and models, and
its entangling network of guiding symbols.

The motif impresses on the reader the necessity to keep on
moving even if it means leaving the familiar behind and taking the
leap into a new beginning and the unknown. "High and Dry" already
warned against settling down with a myopic, complacent view of
life. Accordingly, symbols for such an attitude are rejected--the
lighthouse, anchors, and other easy ways out of the labyrinth of
existence--just as the Ariadne threads and four-leafed clovers are
in The Musical Eel. A life which accepts those symbols and the
attitudes they represent as guidelines for existence is compared
to a life "swollen with compromises" and is emphatically rejected
in the volume Portrait Gallery.[27] Having come close to sharing
the fate of the dried-up starfish in "High and Dry," the speaker
in "Washed Ashore" expresses his desperation in a soliloquy on the
spreading stagnation he perceives all around: "with friends more
and more settling down as lighthouses," he is himself about to be
washed ashore dead. Here, the images used indicate the severity

of the deadlock, the fact that it is a question of life and death:

> (...)
> up with your tongue old boy
> (...)
> with my still effective tongue
> I paddle myself free through flabby seaweeds
>   and clenched breakers
> to the shallow beach where I hitch a ride with
>   Moby Dick
> who is going alongside blowing politely:
> Mister Jonah, I presume?
> With a click of the tongue I take off and jump   on.
> (27)

The decision to leave the familiar sphere of family and friends because it has become synonymous with meaninglessness--with living death--is based on the commitment to develop continuously. It is obviously related to the imperative found in the earlier poems: "speak with your own voice / your first words / goodbye paradise," speak with "unsprayed idioms."[28] By using his tongue to depart from an unbearable state, the speaker here opens another perspective, that of the author's position in society.

The difficulty of the mission is underscored by the biblical allusion to Jonah's responsibility. Like Jonah, the poet is engaged in a struggle to fulfill his responsibility.   The challenge he must face is not to submit to artificial, deluding substitutes as the emperor of China does in Hans Christian Andersen's tale of "The Nightingale." Benny Andersen juxtaposes the case of the sleepless emperor with that of "The Sleepless Poet" ("Den søvnløse digter") to exemplify the two conflicting attitudes which arise among poets.[29] The poet who represses the disquieting aspects of reality by escaping into a l'art pour l'art concept is vehemently opposed by the "raving mad young nightingales" who drown out the artificial bird as they "sing about lost faces" and refuse to be silenced. They symbolize a young generation of poets unwilling to submit to an art defined solely in aesthetic terms. They represent a source of indignation for the poet whose fate is merged with that of the emperor in Hans Christian Andersen's tale:

> Do let me sleep
> bury me with the art bird
> and on the tombstone have inscribed
> Cursed be Hans Christian Andersen.
> But the nightingales move closer
> and sing all night
> Good morning   (10)

Ignoring the authentic corresponds to dying, a process which the "authentic nightingales" are steadily working against. From the point of view of the observing speaker, who this time remains outside the poem, the humorous twist at the poem's end amounts to an expression of an almost malicious pleasure at the success of the authentic birds, at the victory of reality over artificial evasion.

The poem may express, as well, Andersen's understanding of the reductive quality of some of the artistic experimentation undertaken within the concrete poetry movement of the mid to late 1960's in Denmark. Such literary experimentation is exposed as evasive with respect to poetic communication in "The Lazy Poet" ("Den dovne digter"), which consists of a blank page with a period in the lower right-hand corner, and alludes to certain catchy experiments within that movement. Andersen shows that for the poet too, in orienting himself, it is here and now where meaningful communication must take place.

5

The Personality

Departing from the fundamental contrasts--the universal qualities of existence and the individual perspective shaped in a modern, socio-historical context--Andersen pursues the theme of balance by focusing on the many coexisting oppositions that must be consciously dealt with. Since the basic experience of spatial and temporal infinity inspires the individual with admiration but also with a shocking <u>horror vacui</u>, it is not surprising to find a host of support structures generated in society. The reductive, stagnating effect on the personalty--and on society at large-- which is inherent in many strategies for coping and for defining a position in life is exposed in Andersen's poetry. Although Andersen is well known for his depiction of antithetical situations, he is not considered an author who provides solutions. To be sure, his poems continue to raise the questions: how can individual needs be combined with a critical and responsible stance in society? How can the opposing forces of utilitarian integration and the resistance to it be balanced? But many poems do point toward a synthesis, a means of coming to grips with an apparent deadlock, and bear witness to the dialectical thought process which pervades Andersen's work.

The starting point for resolving the rigid opposition is hinted at subtly but frequently throughout the different volumes of poetry, in love poems and lyrical impressions from nature, and in such poems as "This Is," "Life is Narrow and High," and "Monday," to name just a few. It amounts to an ethical imperative to reach out to others and it relies on a heightened consciousness of the destructive value of myopic, self-effacing tactics and it also relies on awareness of the natural and genuine. Rooted in this individual awareness, the responsibility to become ourselves and the obligation to reach out to others prove to be complementary aspects of the process of living fully, at least as fully as appears possible during our "guest performance as jumping-jack."[1] Society's directives versus the challenge "you must find yourself" form a constellation that should lead to the imperative of reaching out, with the individual personality constituting the key for this development. This process is far from the simplistic formula it might appear to be at first glance. On the contrary, the poems constantly point out how difficult in itself it is to recognize self-deceptive attitudes and self-effacing strategies, especially once they have become part of our daily behavior; consequently, it is equally difficult for the speakers in Andersen's poems to find themselves and to know how they can obtain genuine meaning in life. Even if they have managed to come so far as to be conscious of the necessity to be themselves and to reach out, it still remains a major challenge to actually transcend self-protection and make the transition from the "I" to the "you," and ultimately to the perspective of "we." Andersen's poetry emphasizes the fact that no one-time synthesis can be achieved; that instead, oppositions will be encountered constantly and will have to be dealt with and resolved continuously. It is the individual's commitment to this endlessly moving process which constitutes an essential component of the ethical stance of reaching out.

I Isolation

Because the process is continuous, and because it consists of individual variants, Andersen stresses in his poems that he is not supplying advice and easy-to-follow instructions for a so-called proper way of living. He refuses to impose advice on others just as he does not care to be imposed upon himself. "I--who after all more or less know / what it means to be me-- / hardly know how my life ought to be lived-- / how then can other people know it?"[2] The opinion signalled by this poem's speaker parallels a view expressed all along in Andersen's poems: it is difficult for us to live according to an ethical stance, incorporating such ideals as being ourselves and being willing to reach out, when we are already burdened by the effort to keep our own perspective from getting fixed, anchored, inflexible. Andersen formulates the degree of difficulty involved by placing at the center of attention the problems the individual encounters when attempting to break through protective self-isolation and reach out to others in daily situations, as in "Goodness" ("Godhed").

> I've always tried to be good
> it's very demanding
> I'm a real hound for
>   doing something for someone

```
hold coats
  doors
    seats
get someone a job
  or something
open up my arms
let someone have his cry on my shirt
but when I get my chance
I freeze completely
some kind of shyness maybe
I urge myself--do it
fling your arms wide
but it's difficult to sacrifice yourself
    when somebody's watching
so hard to be good
    for more than a few minutes
like holding your breath
however with daily practice
I have worked up to a whole hour
if nobody disturbs me
I sit all alone
with my watch in front of me
spreading my arms
    again and again
no trouble at all
I am actually best
when I'm all alone                          (SP, 37/39)
```

The inhibition which prevents the speaker from making contact reveals his underlying fear of the rejection he might experience if the urge to make a friendly gesture were followed. Although the realization that this problem could be resolved by practice is sensible, the solitary manner in which these sincere exercises in goodness are carried out is absurd. Benny Andersen develops the poem's theme--the individual caught in the circle of an inhibition--in a tripartite monologue: desire, actual state, chosen consequence. This structure corresponds to the "triad principle" on the linguistic level.[3] After building up his character's good intentions by way of accelerated enumeration, Andersen actually stops with "but when I get my chance / I freeze completely." As he continues by describing the moment of ineptitude, he delays any further action, prolonging the moment of immobility to match the comparison "like holding your breath," before he releases the speaker into the hope of practice sessions, leading up to the pseudo-solution in the punch line at the end. In the model presented in this poem, Andersen unmasks the seemingly positive values of good intentions and conscientious practice as counterproductive, in that they are not transferable to the individual's interpersonal relationships and his participation in a group or in society at large. Through the portrayal of comic frustration mixed with an absurd pride in solitary achievements, Andersen may distract somewhat from the basically tragic and unresolved isolation of the poem's speaker. Nevertheless, his immense frustration should stimulate the reader to ask critically for the possible reasons for such a discrepancy between the ideal itself and the speaker's approach to it. As in the poem "It's High Time," Andersen indicates that something has been misrepresented in the speaker's education because "Goodness" too, with its very beginning, points back to childhood and youth. "I've always tried to be good" reads like a reassuring reaction to a parent's or teacher's admonition: be good. The entire poem thus acquires the tenor of a justification--a tenor more commonly developed as a technique in Andersen's short stories. But the justification cannot cover up an inadequacy which the speaker was never taught to overcome; what he apparently was taught was to follow instructions and to practice. The lack of knowledge of how to achieve genuine interaction with others joins with the speaker's fear of taking risks and thus completes the circle of isolation: not only courage is lacking, but also consciousness.

Far from proposing a one-sided criticism which exempts the individual from responsibility for his or her own contribution to the dilemma of such a circle, Andersen has his speaker in a later poem express an opposing reaction to a statement made by Garcin in Sartre's play No Exit that hell is other people: "On the contrary, dear Sartre, / come and look at my hell. / I am standing in a nothingness, / missing my loved ones as never before / and fear the meeting with them."[4] It should be kept in mind here that it is not Sartre, but the coward Garcin who gives the definition of hell Andersen reacts to in this poem; it is Garcin who tries to avoid facing the truth which he learns about himself through others. Similarly to Sartre, Andersen stresses how we first of all create our own hell, tormenting ourselves with isolation, self-pity, and fear of the future. Above all, our many ways of isolating ourselves from others equal evasive tactics as far as being ourselves is concerned; for with respect to being yourself, Andersen warns, "that you are by no means / if you only sit staring at yourself."[5] The central theme in Andersen's poetry--balance in life--is hinged upon the necessity of our finding ourselves to the degree possible and of then being ourselves. Clearly defined above, this effort requires an abrogation of withdrawal from others and demands a shedding of protective shells, an emergence from the psychological hiding places that provide a false sense of security and stability; in short, it means "swallowing your inner Bowler hat" in order "to come to."[6]

II   Authentic Interaction

"Goodness," "The Soul," and other poems describe a number of the difficulties the individual encounters when trying "to come to," to come into existence and be--not merely as an isolated self but there for others, receptive to others. Andersen brings this theme more into the foreground in the 1978 volume Under both Eyes, without, however, continuing in the dramatic style of such earlier poems as "Goodness." Instead, a pensive tone dominates. Consciousness is no longer focused primarily on the speaker's interest

in wanting to be there for others; it is now centered on the wish
to achieve authentic interaction. Alternative approaches for the
<u>right</u> way of genuinely being there for others are weighed against
each other, and the necessity of being there--now and here, where
life goes on--is voiced emphatically. Also stressed is the recognition that not only is it very demanding to be there for others,
but it is also very difficult to provide the best assistance.
Aware of the possible consequences of his choice, the speaker experiences the anguish of choosing responsibly. What is the best,
the right, way to behave toward others? Sticking to a social role
and performing as expected or daring to leave such a role and risk
being rejected? Should a problem be reasoned out or should a comforting, perhaps superficial answer be given? Should a mother be
comforted about her baby's crying at night or be advised to go to
the doctor? ("To a Mother;" "Til en mor").[7] The complexity of
finding a balance when reaching out to others is exemplified in a
poem addressed to a friend who has asked for help, in "To One Who
Threw a Chair" ("Til en der smed en stol"):[8]

> You stood with the chair lifted when I came.
> I was winded.
> You'd telephoned for me.
> Your eyes stood out
> and your teeth when you shouted:
> "Four years of my life I've wasted on her!
> Is there anything so cold as a woman
> who used to be warm?
> For four years I've loved her!"
> I didn't get a chance to say
> anything.
> Then you screamed:
> "Out of my life!"
> and threw the chair.
> Not the window! I scarcely
> had time to think.
> Well, then here's a list
> of what I didn't get to say:
> 1) Four years don't need to be wasted
>   consider them a gift
>   which you might very well have missed
> 2) I have two tickets to Count Basie
> 3) That's just the kind of chair I need myself right now
> 4) Someday we'll have a good laugh over this
> 5) Keep standing there like that so I can get my camera
> 6) Can you lend me a hundred dollars?
> 7) You're holding that chair wrong
> 8) When two mirrors mirror each other
>   do they then mirror their own mirror image
>   or do they mirror the reflection
>   of the other mirror's mirror image?
> 9) Your fly is open
>
> But the most important thing

> was that I got there
> just before the chair was thrown
> and shattered against the wall
> between two windows.
> The most important thing
> is to have a faithful friend
> watching
> when you smash your chair.[9]

The speaker distances the impact of sorrow after having witnessed its violent, angry eruption, by offering a multitude of possibly comforting reactions. They all imply a slightly different attitude toward coping with lost love, as well as toward comforting an afflicted friend; they each may be wrong and may increase the grief. By not giving the speaker the chance to take on any of the listed attitudes, the poem leads us to an awareness that the most responsible way of reaching out is that of sincere, unpretentious presence. Having shown concern for the other through an immediate response, the speaker has arrived just in time to assist as a witness as his friend copes with his changed situation through a relieving burst of anger.

It is the art of living, "the art of coming into the world," Andersen is preoccupied with, a theme which culminates in the sixty-page poem, "Blanket-Toss or The Art of Coming into the World," in the most recent collection by the same title.[10] In this poem, being oneself and reaching out are extended into a modern epos which gives a bird's-eye view of everyday life in this Western industrialized society and of the adult individual's painful effort to be born. With the idiom of "coming into the world," synonymous with being born, Andersen defines the act of living as a process of continuously undergoing an act of birth; this is already hinted at in the early poem "Young" from 1962. In "Young," the vehement objection to social conditioning, mediocrity, and human ossification had been countered by the ethical commitment to reach out and to get other people to do the same; to make them conscious of the scream that is being repressed everywhere was depicted as the beginning of a long and very difficult process of birth: "under heavy labor pains hands come out of pockets."[11] Different aspects of this birth process are rendered in close-up views given in many poems, usually focusing on one of the numerous obstacles that prevent a person from coming into the world--since more than courage is needed: "What confidence lies in those few words / To come into the world / That is / what it is all about."[12]

Confidence is precisely what most of the speakers in Andersen's poems lack, be it self-confidence in what they can offer others, confidence in the reception of their efforts by others, or confidence in their ability to deal with a rejection by others. These glimpses of difficult "labor pains" exemplify once again Andersen's refusal to offer overall solutions; what he does offer is an ethical stance, an affirmative attitude toward living and toward finding the courage to be born over again. He reminds us that it is at least necessary to keep trying and thus be able to reach out and give. By focusing on the relationship between two

people, the smallest social unit, he points out the essential   and
basic   importance   of love for providing the confidence needed for
living.
     The   spirit   of   this   conviction   permeates   the   long   poem
"Blanket-Toss or the Art of Coming into the World," where the main
themes of Andersen's   poetry   come   together   and   form   a   modern
Everyman's   epic.   From   the   setting of a Copenhagen suburb, the
average man's   view   of   the   antithetical   nature   of   the   human
condition--and of Western culture's contradictions in particular--
is represented in   a   space-odyssey   which   is   propelled   by   the
speaker's   raised   consciousness.   As in many of Andersen's poems,
individual loneliness in the face of   existential   reality   determines   the   point   of   view.   The   speaker addresses himself in a
soliloquy which at the same time permits him to step out of, reach
out   of, the isolation that encloses him.   He can thus establish a
close relationship with the reader or the   listener,   to   whom   he
transmits   his   personal   perspective   on a widely shared problem.
The fear he expresses at the poem's outset is a   fundamental   one,
the fear of losing the woman he loves.   For him, such a loss would
have far-reaching effects since he has defined   his   identity   and
meaning in life in relation to her.

                    It is there when you reach out your hand
                    It is there when you don't reach out your hand
                    the moss on the stone
                    the nameplate on the door
                    your lover's face
                    it is there when you reach out your hand
                    It is there
                    and it is not there
                    It is there
                    and you are not there
                    (...)
                    You can see that plate with the name
                    you can spell the name
                    you know it by heart
                    You read it again and again
                    imprint your name in your mind
                    You dare not turn around
                    At the moment you turn around
                    the name
                    the plate
                    the door
                    the house
                    the world
                    are maybe gone
                    (...)
                    If need be you can learn to live with
                    closing your eyes to the problem
                    of the moss under your fingernails
                    of the name on the plate on the door
                    but the face
                    that face
                    you love above all

```
her beloved face
the warm eyes which embrace you
the fearless smile which is turned toward you
It is there when you reach out your hand
(...)
It is there
and it is not there
It is there
and you are not there
That you cannot go along with
But that which you cannot go along with
makes you afraid to turning around
afraid of losing the most beloved
and the fear to lose the most beloved
makes it unreal while you stare at it
It is not there while you are there
you are there while you are not there
unbelievable
but not for that reason true.
Is the whole thing only imagination
where is that imagination coming from
or what do you imagine
It can come to the point that you turn around
It can come to the point that your fear
of turning around changes
to a fear of not turning around
```

```
You turn around
It has come to that point.[13]
```

The severity of the experience of losing genuine love--and thus losing   ground   in   life--is conveyed through the speaker's disquieting fear and doubts and is accentuated by means of a motif familiar from Orpheus in the Underworld. Like Orpheus, the speaker has reached the point where he feels compelled to turn around for reassurance.   Looking back to his small world down the street, only to see it fade suddenly as the sun draws behind a cloud, he undergoes a   severe   shock, losing all feeling in the arm that is reaching out.   This is followed by the loss of weight, shadow and laughter--the   complementary   aspects   of his identity; literally losing the ground he is standing on, he floats upward to embark on an involuntary journey.   It is the moment of dizziness encountered so often in Andersen's poems, the existential experience of losing ground and being tossed into consciousness, comparable to Roquentin's spells in Nausea,[14] until the momentary spell passes--until he   finds   himself standing in his neighborhood holding on to a light-pole.
     The symbolic quality of his odyssey into world and space lies in   its   demonstration of the significance of love and confidence, the essential and most meaningful qualities in life, with respect to both the individual's existential experience and his confronta-tions with society.   Through their life-giving property,   the speaker   overcomes his fears and dizziness and at the poem's

climax, regains his balance in a birth process, comes into the
world and home. Within this frame, his bird's eye view of Western
civilization provides shocking glimpses of an environment determined by an inhuman concept of progress. Motifs from earlier Andersen poems are resumed as the speaker sketches contradictions in
human actions and the resulting threats to the quality of life.
The two reactor towers of Barsebäck, the atomic power station on
the Swedish coast across from Copenhagen, are depicted as the
modern twin temples of a civilization that adores technological
progress.   Its ideology has left its marks on the environment in
the form of various catastrophes generated by competitive exploitation: among them, chemical pollution and oil-spills. They
are in blatant contrast with the humanitarian efforts of the Red
Cross in underdeveloped areas which suffered from natural
catastrophes and cannot escape those of civilization either.
Violation of the environment is paralleled by human aggression, be
it through hijacking mid-air, in traffic situations among angry
drivers, or in the deathly competitive race of people against each
other that is essentially directed at shortening their own lives.
Andersen projects the environment's hostility toward children
through an uncanny vision of a future "museum of children." A poem
by that title had already touched the problem in the socio-
critical collection Here on the Reserve, as had "Escapism" from
The Musical Eel , where the motif was emphatically linked with a
narrow-minded notion of progress.   Repulsed by a civilization
whose sanctioned consumer attitude reduces other people to objects, the speaker's decreasing hope--his eschatological
consciousness--can only be countered and balanced by love and confidence. Love and confidence enable him in the end to carry out
his birth-process after he has seen a broad spectrum of suffering
in the world; that is precisely why his answer to a routine question, when he arrives home at the end of the poem, assumes another
dimension of meaning: "her voice / in the middle of everything: /
'Is it you?' / You answer: / 'Yes!'" (75) The model of love in
the smallest social unit is presented as a model to be developed
further in a larger context. Potentially, love is there all the
time, but confidence is needed for developing it and for meeting
it when someone is reaching out to offer it.[15]

   Symbols for love--and for its qualities warmth and joy--like
the sun and the flowers, recur throughout Andersen's poems including the songs in Above Certain Waters;[16] they constitute"the
whole thing"--all that basically counts--and have many models in
nature. "What should we do without nature," Andersen had ex-
claimed earlier in the poem "Swamp" ("Mose"), in Portrait Gallery
and the poem "Love" (Kærligheden"), from The Inner Bowler Hat, had
clearly shown nature's model function.[17]

> Love
> does not hang on trees
> but it is them you look at
> when you miss it
> I wonder how they manage
> standing so far away from each other
> barely able to reach the next tree

```
            with the tip of a leaf
            and that tree is maybe
                    not the right one at all
            but rather in the way
                    still they grow daily
            and here you walk around in the forest
                    on your mobile roots
            you stick your mobile branches in your pockets
                    that is the least
            and rush back into town.
```

The requirement to utilize our potential is the imperative hidden between the lines here, as Andersen points to our habit of hiding instead of reaching out. Shaped by his consciousness of the important yet neglected details that form our habits and frequently deform our attitudes, Andersen's ethical stance as a poet consists of bringing into focus those aspects of daily life which have become so automatic for us that we have lost sight of their implications. Becoming aware of them represents the essential first step in learning to cope with large-scale difficulties.

The often varied message of Andersen's poetry emerges in a dialectical pattern which can be summed up as follows: to find oneself--to genuinely develop a personality and be--requires realistic self-acceptance and full recognition of life's complexities; it requires, as well, an open-minded and sincere approach to others that can serve as the basis for the confidence needed in facing the possible risks entailed. It is not so much taking the right action--which after all may be difficult if not impossible to discern--that counts; rather, it is, to speak with both Kierkegaard and Sartre, the continuous choice in itself that counts.[18] Andersen's dialectic restates the fundamental question of "to be or not to be" and stresses that, in any case, it is necessary to be here and now, to be receptive to others and, above all, sincere. Such a stance involves living with both eyes open, to use a recurring motif; or--to go all the way back to the ethical and literary program formulated in The Musical Eel--it calls upon us to absorb "the shocks from far away detonations through our feet and let them unfold as caresses and open eyes."[19] In brief, this program encompasses Benny Andersen's central themes and shapes, as well, the technique of close-up focus that he uses so effectively in numerous variations and perspectives in his lyric poetry.

6

Recording "The Other Reality": The Short Stories

In both theme and structure, Andersen's two short story collections The Pillows and Fats Olsen and Other Stories reflect the antithetical pattern we have observed in his poetry. Since emphasis in the stories lies primarily on the problematic confrontations the individual experiences in society, the narrative strategy is characterized by a striking seriousness in the sense that being "a citizen in the land of the smile" is truly not funny at all.

Andersen's focus lies almost exclusively on young or middle-aged men at a critical point in their lives. They are so-called "small men" who suddenly find themselves in situations that force them to act differently and disrupt their everyday routine. The struggle they are seen engaged in quite often takes on the dimensions of a power struggle beween two or more people, but even then it is largely the protagonist's battle with himself. This battle determines the structural pattern of the stories and builds on a common thematic denominator: the individual's struggle for meaning in life. Thematic exposition is carried out in a manner similar to the tripartite structure observed in a number of Andersen's poems. In the narrative context, however, it is more clearly carried beyond the protagonist's chosen solution to the conflict between his actual and desired state of existence, with intimations of the grim consequences of his choice. By thus revealing the self-deceptive aspect of the protagonist's solution, Andersen destroys the illusion of a valid dialectical structure. It is usually the first person narrator, who in an effort to justify his evasive strategy tries most persuasively to project the validity of what might be termed the action's pseudo-dialectic course.

Andersen's first collection is characterized by the thematic and structural similarities among the stories, and by the markedly growing thematic intensity that culminates in the Surrealistic title story "The Pillows" ("Puderne") at the end of the volume. This intensity is rooted in the programmatic universal challenge to find out about life, and thus about himself, which the young man in the initial story "The Break-Up" ("Bruddet") had accepted. The subsequent stories demonstrate how the protagonists have neglected to accomplish this task because they have settled for only a partial solution: the mere daily functioning in a well-organized routine. This neglect, this obvious inability to cope with that fundamental challenge, constitutes the major source for the visibly increased seriousness in the plots. When these protagonists suddenly are confronted with "the other reality" that seemed to have been so well repressed and integrated,[1] questions arise about the less obvious reasons for their handicap. In view of this thematic continuity, the parenthetical function of the first and last story catches the reader's eye, for within this frame Andersen presents a spectrum of substitutions with which his protagonists structure their everyday lives in order to maintain their emotional balance. The title of the volume therefore underscores symbolically the fact that they seek refuge in a functional system of compensations, in a world of pillows to fall back on.

The conflicts and contradictions in which Andersen's protagonists become entangled derive from their cultural environment, which conditions them to integrate themselves as well-functioning members of society and thereby prevents them from developing the awareness necessary for self-realization. It is therefore no accident that Andersen's first volume of short fiction opens with a story like "The Break-Up." In accordance with the development in his second and third collection of poetry, he no longer uses nature as a catalyst but interpersonal conflict when he formulates the necessity of individual consciousness about life's enigmas along with the imperative to find a personal stance. Many of the subsequent stories exemplify the problems of a search for an individual personality by pointing out how the protagonists have settled for, or tend to stick with, a mere social identity. Such an identity is--at least in part--already imprinted during childhood and adolescence and readily available through adherence to prescriptive norms and to continued pressures to conform. For this reason, a sincere ethical stance is often seen combined with evasive strategies leading to easy ways of finding a place in society rather than the protagonist's success in finding himself. Other stories depict the human catastrophe when such an existential question has not been resolved and a meaningful participation in society is obstructed for the individual. Nor is society left unscathed; it is presented critically as utilitarian, property-oriented, and thus instrumental in decreasing the quality of life by promoting a slavish and all-pervasive consumer attitude.

The basic theme, a search for meaning, covers a range of motifs centering on the struggle for self-respect and the interpersonal contact necessary for a happy and fulfilled existence. This endeavor requires a critical awareness of the norms society offers for self-realization and interaction among its members. It is precisely this awareness which the protagonists lack, whereas the reader is guided to perceive not only this dilemma but also the flaws of society's normative concepts. When the protagonist relies on these norms, he is misdirected in his search for meaning and further intraps himself through his blind acceptance of the way these norms are presented to him. In exposing this situation, Andersen works as a social critic who is amusing in an alarming way. To what extent he engages in social satire in his stories and provides "a reader's cabaret" for us, as the Swedish critic Lars Grahn has suggested,[2] remains to be seen when considering the conflicts presented in these stories. This quality is linked with the protagonists' chosen strategies to get ahead in their struggles, and it cannot be overlooked how heroic an effort they invest in these strategies. But most of Andersen's main characters are negative heroes, often nameless and representing human types; caught in their predicament, they clearly present a challenge to the reader: to balance sympathy with critical awareness without feeling superior or exempt from the underlying problems depicted in these scenes from the everyday life of our modern society.

I The Challenge

With its theme of the individual's struggle for meaning, the initial story "The Break-Up" has a programmatic value for the entire collection. It constitutes one of its very few optimistic examples, since the protagonist is about to transcend his stage of dependency on others. The story presents a young man's description of his struggle to escape the greyness of his existence. He is portrayed as leading a vicarious life pieced together from newspaper t opics everyone gets upset about and cliche opinions about interesting vacation spots everyone is talking about; taken together, they reflect a need for something special, as generally advertised in the media, to substitute for a missing vital element in daily life. Accordingly, the void and dissatisfaction he feels are superficially associated with a lack of unusual experiences. When his former geometry teacher points out to him the small paradoxes in life that are visible all around, he does not realize that, if only he were aware he, too, could perceive the unusual which is happening here and now around him. Instead, he channels his longing for new orientation and meaning in life into a longing for the mythical entity "life;" he expects to gain full view of it some day through his mentor and then be saved from an unfulfilling routine existence.

> Nothing interested me; I never went to the movies,
> did not get outside a door, stopped getting
> together with my girlfriend because she reminded

me too much about everything now and here, this
area I was sick of, spring which let things happen
and buds open up, but not for me, all those small
inclinations and habits that had marked off my existence until now but which I was ready to deny
the moment he snapped his fingers and said:
'Let's take off!' And finally, she and I could not
talk to each other any more at all since the conversation came to a halt because I couldn't stand
talking in the usual words and clichés, and
because new ones had not come in yet, and the
relationship gradually fell apart.[3]

Withdrawal from the everyday, waiting to be served the whole
truth, proves to be a form of escapism preventing the narrator
from realizing that individual awareness is needed to perceive how
life is taking place around him with all its seemingly peculiar
manifestations and idiosyncracies. His passivity is indicative of
his having been conditioned to a consumer mentality which he is
still unable to shed. He transfers it to the person responsible
for his awakening to this semi-conscious state of mind. His one-
time teacher, an outside figure who earns his living as private
tutor all over town, plays the dubious role of friend and mentor
while himself trying to figure out his life. Not only does he in-
troduce his former pupil to life's contradictions and complexity;
his own personality itself opposes accepted clichés about
mathematicians, for he projects the image of an unsettled person,
far removed from a systematically calculable view of existence.
Although he offers no guidelines beyond pointing out that life
consists of an immense spectrum of opposites, from Dostoevsky's
"underground man" to Mozart's "luminous rooms," his young friend
clings to the illusion of being prepared by his mentor for the
solution to life's enigma--for the synthesis of all these conflicting truths he was given a glimpse of. What the teacher underestimates are the odds he is working against, the fact that his
young friend--conditioned by society's directives and
prefabricated notions of normality--expects, as a normal consequence, a systematic conclusion to the partial insights he was
given.

In addition, the teacher's withdrawal into silence when the
conversation turns superficial, does nothing to eliminate
triviality from their dialogue, but supports the myth of a special
meaning waiting to be unveiled in the near future. With its illusion of harmony and security, society's myth of normality continues its sway and proves to be an effective conditioning because
it has not been recognized as a manipulating force that is an artificial construct and capable of being changed. The young man
has been conditioned so thoroughly that he keeps awaiting directives and merely consumes the books and records he is given, accepting them theoretically and emotionally only insofar as they
promise to reveal life's purpose and give him an ultimate meaning
which he still lacks. It never occurs to him to open his eyes for
parallels around him, to develop his sensitivity, or even to consider that his mentor might be in a very similar position of

searching for meaning. Consequently, he feels betrayed when his mentor suddenly announces his departure from the city and refuses to take him along, even states he does not know him. The double meaning of this statement, which alludes to a still underdeveloped personality, remains unnoticed. Moreover, the young man must feel justified in his urge to avenge himself, at least at the peak of his feelings of betrayal.

The physical struggle to hang on down by the harbor therefore signifies a struggle necessary to free himself from the older friend--to cut the umbilical cord and start experiencing life independent of outside opinions. Yet, he does not free himself consciously; slightly drunk, and feeling betrayed and disappointed, he is moved to revenge by a part of his individuality that had remained submerged during their long talks. What he experiences as irrational--pushing his mentor off the quay into the water--amounts to an action genuinely motivated by feelings he can call his own for the first time. This unintentioned ending of a friendship means the end of his "hanging on like a bur" (17), his parasitic attitude of living off of his friend's feelings and observations. It represents the beginnings of self-involvement, a willingness to face the challenge: "Feel something yourself (...) Find out about things yourself."(18)

The story's young protagonist brings to mind the protest voiced in the poem "Young," against the effects of society's conditioning to mediocrity, to a life "without really growing or wilting."[4] The vehemence of that poem's protest is paralleled in "The Break-Up" by the difficulty of developing critical consciousness and a genuine personality. The beginning protest visible in the story is still measured by accepted definitions of normality and therefore experienced as an irrational urge for revenge which seeks its target in a friend and mentor who has not fulfilled the expectations his silence seemed to promise: salvation from the lack of meaning sensed as boredom in everyday existence. This irrational urge, however, initiates an act of birth for the young narrator: "But when he was about to stumble over a mooring hawser, my head was suddenly filled with these sharp things so I was about to scream. With a leap, I was by his side and gave him a push over the edge."(18) The criminal aspect of his semiconscious liberation symbolizes the extraordinary efforts needed for a new beginning. No tragic, but far-reaching personal consequences are the result; the story ends with the moral decision: "I am going to find out about something myself." (19)

With its quality of a parable, the story expands, in the familiar context of adolescence, a theme we have seen before in poems, such as "Life" and "Astray:" that Life ought to be lived in "mid-stream" here and now in the everyday situation, not by withdrawal into a state of futile waiting for "the full insight" which might emerge from the fog as "the saving river bank."[5] It is imperative to find out about oneself, life, and meaning in the daily environment, a demanding task exemplified by the subsequent stories.

The idealistic young man in the story "The Intercom" ("Hustelefonen") is confronted with an established adult world that does not take him seriously. He therefore has to strike a

careful balance between his wish to be accepted and his personal
ethics in order to avoid integrating himself into a meaningless
hierarchy. Andersen depicts this conflict by pointing out one of
the common barricades people erect in everyday life. A means of
diminishing personal communication, the newly installed inter-
office telephone symbolizes an emphasis on professional hierarchy
at the expense of concern about colleagues in the work place.
Motivated by self-interest, the head clerk added it in a move to
keep Toft, his colleague next in rank, at a distance in the adja-
cent office. Narrated from Henrik's perspective at the bottom of
this office hierarchy, the story illustrates the importance of
personal communication in the effect the intercom has on him, the
office boy who works as an apprentice during the day while continuing his education in night courses. For Henrik, as well as
for his supervisor Toft and the head clerk, communication is intimately connected with their self-respect and with the importance
they see in their roles at work. While the intercom signifies
distinction for the head clerk, it means a reduction for the other
two because it demonstrates that personal contact with them is not
valued, only their efficient functioning on the job. Toft expresses his bitterness about such devaluation with an ironic sug-
gestion: "Imagine that we had a mirror standing here between us,
right under the Coca-Cola-calendar, so we could see each other's
face when looking into it. Then we wouldn't need to look at each
other, we could simply look into the mirror, wouldn't that be use-
ful?" (23) Toft's exaggeration indicates his criticism of a tendency to let efficiency take precedence over human contact, over
the personal feelings expressed in daily small talk which is un-
profitable from a strict business perspective.

While Toft protests verbally against the reduction of individuality to a one-dimensional functional level, stressing that
he had preferred this small company because its size seemed to
guarantee a more humane environment, Henrik had been reacting all
along against the adult established world's indifference by
wearing a bow tie. It appears to be only a weakness that he has
trouble getting up in the morning, habitually forgets to put on
his bow tie, and ends up in the department store across from his
office to buy a new one almost every day. Although he dislikes
bow ties, particularly the cheap affordable ones, wearing them has
become a point of honor for him despite his suspicion that no one
at the office would notice if he forgot to wear it. What seems to
be idiosyncratic, almost compulsive behavior actually amounts to a
desperate attempt at self-persuasion. He refuses to believe in
people's indifference toward him, especially since he is trying so
hard to be an acceptable adult in the eyes of his supervisor Toft.
All his activities are primarily devoted to self-development, to
becoming a respected person, especially from an ethical point of
view. He realizes that something is wrong with his strategy, that
his notes on how his superiors should not have acted have been
useless to prevent his own mistakes, but he cannot figure out that
his concern about being taken seriously prevents him from seeing
more than a conflict of interest between his two superiors. Instead of acting, he only reacts. At a hypersensitive stage in his
development, he is not yet able to balance the oppositions he is

witnessing.   Consequently,   he refuses to join Toft in boycotting
the intercom because he realizes too late that Toft's clumsy   way
of contacting him was not intended as an insult.   Ironically, the
two people who are concerned about genuine personal   communication
cannot   get together.   The extent to which the inhibitions on both
sides contribute to the general atmosphere of indifference is symbolized by the fact that the next day, Henrik's missing bow tie
goes unnoticed; what prevails is a mask of friendly acceptance of
the new situation.   Henrik's desperate gesture at the end of the
story--he runs over to the department store to buy a cheap neck
tie--is directed against the indifference he encounters but
refuses to accept.   It signifies his rather helpless attempt to
revolt against the frustrating situation brought about by the intercom.

II Substitutions

Using average situations as settings,   Andersen   concentrates
on the negative hero, sketching the discrepancies between ideals
and reality and the importance of knowing oneself as a step toward
defining an ethical stance for the interaction with others.   Importance and difficulty of this step are especially seen in Andersen's stories, where the majority of his heroes choose strategies
to live by in an attempt to overcome the obstacles that confront
them in the everyday routine of their lives.   Their endeavors are
directed toward being the person society wants and will accept.
Pressured by conventions,   they manage to conform by achieving a
daily balance and apparent control over their existence.   What
they have neglected, to develop a genuine identity, proves to be
detrimental in crises when this neglect threatens their emotional
balance and continues to lead to pseudo-solutions.
In the story "Distinctive Mark" ("Særpræg"),   such a crisis
occurs when the hero suddenly becomes aware of a potential
catastrophe for his happiness.   Threatened by the fact that he
looks so nondescript as to be indistinguishable from many others
and that his wife likes him that way, he fears that he is easily
replacable by other men in the crowd.   The wide-spread, strictly
material criteria in valuing people, which his reasoning reveals
are confirmed by his social environment.   They determine his
myopic view of himself, make him appear reduced to an object with
certain undistinguished looks and a set of qualities for conforming in accord with accepted social norms.   Based on this view,
he generates equally myopic strategies to secure his happiness.
To achieve the slight distinctive mark, the facial trait
which will distinguish him without changing him, he undergoes a
series of comical and rather futile training methods inspired by
advertisements for body-building.   The constant practice in front
of a mirror, where he frowns in various ways for hours, is intended to achieve the expression of a distinguished personality.
This practice points to an underlying consumer attitude which
takes on grotesque dimensions when he desperately changes his
methods.

> The face is the soul's mirror. Now and then, you
> see faces which in their specific features and
> proportions do not differ from the majority but
> are nevertheless distinguished by something
> unusual, something in their glance, a kind of
> radiance which must come from inside, from behind
> the outer face, from a center of inner strength
> that must be formed and strengthened by powerful
> inner experiences, prolonged thinking, heavy
> scruples, great resignation. I quickly went that
> way, got myself books about foreign religions and
> ancient mystics, crammed the great philosophers
> from Plato to Kierkegaard late at night. In the
> beginning, I was still too impatient. Each time I
> grasped a great thought which pulled away the
> ground from under my present way of life, I darted
> over to the mirror to see if the emotional turmoil
> had not left its mark on me. Each time, I went
> back to the desk equally disappointed and took
> hold of the next inner crisis. (60)

While his readings admittedly undermine the kind of life he has
led up to this point and should--but do not--lead him to revise
his outlook on life, his accelerated and superficial consumption
of them indicates the degree of his desperation. He does not accept life's inherent uncertainty, which precludes the control of
happiness he aspires to, nor does he realize the serious lack of
ethical values which supports an all-inclusive consumer mentality
that might be termed a modern kind of cannibalism. His absurd
strategies may be amusing for the detached observer; at the same
time, it is pathetic to witness the either futile or nerve-racking
techniques he devises in his struggle for salvation from his insecurity about his wife. The grotesquely overstated importance of
these techniques corresponds to the severity of the feared loss;
for the narrator, losing his wife would be the equivalent of
losing his meaning in life, and thus more severe than merely
losing ground in the way he has lived so far, which, after all, is
widely accepted. For him, meaning in life is obviously connected
with the structure he has given it through his marriage. Consequently it is the sudden factual uncertainty about the possible
love-affair his wife might have had with a well known charmer that
causes him to develop the distinguished appearance, the unfortunately somewhat unpredictable and transitory nervous tick. The
distorted values already visible in his various tactics are in-
stantly confirmed by his environment: his popularity increases at
home, at work, at parties; respect along with self-confidence follow naturally, as do job promotion and happiness.

The implied criticism of a superficially created meaning
linked with equally superficial concepts of happiness and security
heightens at the end of the story when it becomes obvious that,
with this kind of happiness, meaning in life has been achieved,
leaving the protagonist with no other goal to live for. The artificial quality of this controlled happiness is exposed further
since it hinges upon the nervous tick alone and therefore requires

perpetuation. Only in his early thirties, the protagonist has already reduced himself to a neurotic person, constantly generating
new horror phantasies about losing his wife in order to preserve
his "tick frequency," and thus upholding the social myths he lives
by. His concluding question concerning what could possibly be
done about his ticks--though a rhetorical question in the dialogue
with his wife--stresses the actual need for a reassessment of social norms and values. This story's critical impact is heightened
by the fact that the salvation mechanisms are not only employed
but rewarded.

Clinging to a certain way of life has become the artificial
life saver for many of Andersen's heroes, the means by which they
create a substitute for the lack of meaning they sense in a life
where human development and relationships are determined by market
values. Sex as a substitute for love to counter-balance loneliness symbolizes this tendency in the story "Kill those Bantam
Chickens" ("Kværg de dværghøns"). The dreary existence in the
chicken coop is juxtaposed with people's night-long party life and
their strenuous efforts to gloss over their otherwise monotonous
everyday existence.

From the perspective of the first person narrator, a fat
middle-aged woman who plays the role of party jester, a critical
distance is maintained because her obesity assigns her a position
outside of the usual competition for sexual companionship. Only
this outsider role grants Trille her inclusion at the parties and
allows her to voice the detached yet sharp criticism of the
behavior she observes. The milieu she sketches for her girlfriend
Annie is characterized by heavy drinking and by intense sexual activity which are indicative of certain social myths about living
fully by enjoying the "high life," and filling an entire night
with heated discussions, music, and amorous adventures. The con-
traints and disappointments of the week are exchanged on Saturday
night for the desire to make up for an unfulfilled everyday existence. The substitute nature of this behavior is evident when
spouses pair up with someone else behind each others' backs.
While a young wife discussed South Africa, for example, "her husband managed to climb up two light poles, munch several hyacinth
bulbs, take Gerda out into the coat closet for fifteen minutes--it
was she, by the way, who hung on a clothes hanger when we had to
get our coats in the morning--after which he came back and barged
in on the middle of a discussion about the European Common Market
System by saying: Einstein was good enough! and fell into a
stupor behind the piano with an iron sculpture over him." (42)
There is no doubt about the consumer aspect of these desperate efforts to make life more meaningful through excitement, even if
there is mutual agreement among spouses, an attitude Trille
evaluates as "crazy in an honest way." By contrast, she exposes
Preben--one of the clique--as a seducer who uses drunk girls like
objects in order to build up his image as Don Juan in a constant
need to prove himself successful and restore his self-respect
because his wife has left him.

Trille's account of such substitution efforts is effectively
juxtaposed with her half depressed, half angry remarks about her
girlfriend's bantam rooster: "Once every twenty minutes, he

shuffles up onto one of the hens like onto the scales; three
seconds afterwards, he gets off and wallows away complacently
while the hen shakes herself a little and goes on scraping." (40)
The analogy between the male-female party relationships and the
conduct in the chicken coop makes blatantly clear how reduced a
life prevails under the cover of party fun.

Despite her observations, Trille is equally dependent on
these parties. Although she stands apart from the mythical rites
of sexual self-renewal, she needs the feeling of superiority that
her role as critic grants her; and she needs the physical exhaus-
tion after having been up and involved all night long:

> You drink and put on an act for a whole night,
> talk and hear a lot of nonsense, and suddenly it's
> daylight, you haven't slept and aren't sleepy,
> only your tongue feels like emery cloth, and then
> coffee comes, real people's coffee, it can almost
> make you religious! Glasses and guests are lying
> all around, only three or four are left with blank
> eyes and beer on their clothes, someone manages to
> get croissants and rolls from around the corner;
> you sniff and bite into the buns, you have sur-
> vived, you are whole and round, arms and legs are
> roughly where they usually are, your clothes are
> just a little wrinkled, you drink your coffee,
> your heart kicks up like an old circus horse, and
> then out into the air, that's the most magnificent
> part--the haze, drenched branches in the gardens,
> birds stare at you with big surprised eyes, (...)
> I always feel freshly bathed all the way through
> and go straight home and to bed, wake up four
> hours later all alone without a hangover, think
> that I'll be out visiting you in the afternoon,
> (...) and make myself cosy until I have to leave.
> (44)

It is the feeling of having survived that counts. Everyone seeks
to get out of these parties the sense of an immense achievement
necessary for coping with another week. Also, Trille's girlfriend
Annie, who is never included, is dependent on Trille's reports
each Sunday in order to live vicariously. For both of them, it
compensates for their loneliness. Trille's account is especially
shocking because of the matter-of-fact attitude with which she integrates herself and Annie into the kind of market she has
described. Whether she considers it a fair trade to help Preben
get over his problems by sleeping with him or whether she advises
Annie to stay slim and promises to get her someone on a vacation
to Southern Europe, she clearly follows market norms. All the
story's participants are immersed in substituting for a lack of
genuine fulfillment; they have accepted a compensatory way of life
and the social myths along with it.

III Underdevelopment and Overreaction

Focusing on the smallest social unit, the married couple, Andersen illustrates how fiercely the battle for happiness can be
conducted. In "The Hot-Water Bottle" ("Varmedunken"), an almost
Strindbergian rivalry is acted out between the partners. Narrated
from the husband's point of view in the manner of self-
justification, the story presents his aggressive, self-righteous
reversal of values which he defends to suit his needs. He assumes
the agreement of the reader when he complains about the invasion
of his privacy. He had displayed his good-will, his "common
decency" by agreeing with his wife to temporarily take in an
elderly woman refugee to share their efficiency apartment. His
charity complies with ethical norms, yet only to a certain degree.
When the elderly woman suffers an emotional collapse and has to be
confined to the bed in the couple's room, his charity suddenly is
reversed into cruelty. Since husband and wife have had to shift
their private sphere to kitchen and bathroom for half a year with
no immediate change in sight, the narrator might find sympathizers
who also consider the situation an imposition on the marriage, but
his attitude and the method he employs to get rid of the woman are
far from justified. Filling the hot-water bottle with icy water,
opening the window to gusty cold winds, turning the radio up full
blast, and filling her coffee cup with soap amounts to an inhuman
treatment carried out strategically. What he practices on a small
scale in his efficiency apartment resembles cold-war tactics
familiar from international political conflicts. His strategy of
psychological warfare is aimed at making their guest what he terms
"really ill," that is, so physically ill that she will require
hospitalization. His refusal to grant her the care and support
she so desperately needs--which his wife, by contrast, is eager to
provide--illustrates how values such as peace and harmony are per-
verted to serve egocentric interests: "Why should her sad fate
affect our small peaceful world? (...) It is either us or her.
We are still young and healthy, but she steals all our vigor and
vitality, so we'll end up just as sick and helpless as she is.
I'm doing it for our sake." (31-33)
        The right to a carefree and fulfilling life as proclaimed
here reflects an attitude of social Darwinism. The insistence on
a human right to health and happiness that excludes those who ob-
struct the smooth life style of the more fortunate reveals a
distorted sense of moral values. This distortion for the sake of
justifying a self-serving, possessive attitude culminates in the
narrator's argumentation about love: "To love a person means to
prefer that person so much to all others that they can jump in the
lake. And if they do impose themselves, they must be kicked out
of the way." (34) It is not simply jealousy which motivates this
definition but a narrow-minded concept of cozyness based on seclu-
sion. Because he is too self-conscious to share his marital
privacy, he clings to it, guarding it jealously as his, regardless
of the fact that his wife thinks differently. For him, his
original charity degenerates into a question of territorial rights
he ruthlessly intends to defend. In his view, there are clear-cut

norms to be followed: having extended temporary hospitality, he
now expects institutions to take over, and he refuses to see his
wife's perspective that instead, loving personal caring is needed
in a situation where human nature resists the norms for social
behavior. Nor is he motivated by conviction either when he
finally returns to his former kindness but by the fear of losing
his wife through his inhuman tactics, never realizing what she
demonstrates all along: that sharing her happiness increases it.
With their contrasting attitudes, husband and wife thus compete in
cancelling each other's treatment of their guest.

     To merely classify the narrator as self-centered would,
however, be a simplification; rather, he has to be considered underdeveloped, lacking the autonomy an ethical stance of genuine
love and generosity can grant. Such a stance would presuppose
having defined a meaning in life which transcends the narrow
sphere of personal interest, especially the attitude of having the
right of ownership in his private sphere. His self-centered
reversal of values resulting from the lack of such a stance is
symbolized in the story on one hand by the hot-water bottle with
its icy contents, and on the other by the adverse effect of his
strategy on their guest. The refugee's emotional rather than her
physical state has suffered from the narrator's actions and from
their conditioning effect; she can no longer distinguish his
resumed friendliness from his previous cruel tactics. The extreme
example chosen for this story stresses the necessity for creating
a humane and balanced climate on the small scale of daily interaction in the private sphere, as well as the fundamental importance
of coming to terms with oneself.

     Thematically related to this story is "The Family Friend"
("Husvennen"), another triangle drama, in which the young husband
is unable to establish a genuine and balanced friendship with
their mutual friend. This inability and the resulting insecurity
reveal a person afraid of being himself, whose actions therefore
are determined by the wishes of others. The basic task to be
faced, development of a balanced personality, is more directly addressed in "The Matches" ("Tændstikkerne"). In this story, the
protagonist suddenly leaves home and wanders all over town for two
weeks in order to find his identity once and for all and then stop
with his development. "After all, no one says you should develop
all your life--I, in any case, was developed sufficiently during
the time I was together with my wife." (56) The development his
wife is credited with, however, is based on superficial values
which cannot help solve his identity problem. Through their possessive and evasive behavior these protagonists indicate a lack of
awareness concerning both their egocentricity and their indolence
which prevent them from developing toward a mature, responsible
individuality.

IV Consciousness

Another fraction of a positive outlook presented in the first part of The Pillows can be seen in "Ice-floes in the Baltic" ("Isforekomster i Østersøen"). Here individual loneliness, indifference, and coldness among people are brought to awareness through the focus on communication barriers between the narrator and his young taxi driver. During their odyssey through Copenhagen on a cold March night, both he and the young driver attempt to overcome the superficiality of talking past one another by trying to switch from meaningless remarks about the weather to a more personal conversation. Wishing to be helpful toward the young man, the narrator is hampered by his self-consciousness and by his insistence on walking back to town when he has run out of money because they have driven too far. The barrier is only broken because the young taxi driver finally overcomes his shyness, forgets any business interests, and reaches out to the other by picking him up for a free ride back to town: "'That was dumb of me earlier,' he said. 'You can just as well ride along part of the way, I have to drive in anyway.'" (75) The straight forward honesty of this remark makes no further conversation necessary but has created a relaxed atmosphere, since both have given up their artificial fronts and know it: one has managed to reach out, and the other has managed to accept it. The complementary aspects of contact have been realized here.

The necessity of consciousness about severely impoverished human relationships is emphasized in the second part of The Pillows. In "The Telephone Call" ("Opringningen") and "The Drowning" ("Den druknende")--the only two stories narrated from a more detached third person perspective--a chance appears for changing dangerously fixed states of mind and habits. Death functions as a warning and leads to sudden awareness of an existing coldness or even estrangement among people with a focus on the smallest social unit of marriage. Life has been impoverished to a one-dimensional routine alternating between work and relaxation and has led to a concentration on necessities without a surplus of time and feelings for others. Communication, even in the domestic sphere, has degenerated into a fixed system of habits including a stock of stereo-typical questions and answers, functional for the everyday routine but also a cause of petty irritations the moment one of the spouses ignores these rules established by habit. Life in these relationships resembles a state of petrification in which warmth and genuine personal feelings are no longer shared; instead, they are kept far inside by each partner while their surroundings have consistently turned colder.

Andersen uses a device employed frequently in the contemporary short story, the bewildering enigmatic event which suddenly confronts the protagonist with a hidden or repressed dimension of existence and leaves a sense of imminent danger.[6] The sensation that something is about to die completely, takes on a concrete shape in "The Drowning." Villy, the main character, has isolated himself in his summer cottage by the coast to work on balancing his accounts. Suddenly his fixed routine is thrown off balance when, during a sleepless night, he thinks he sees a human figure drowning off the beach. He also physically loses the ground under his feet when looking for the body the next day. Through the shock of accidentally falling into the water, his sensitivity is reactivated, and he is able to transfer his concrete experience to the state of his marriage. He realizes how he himself and above all his wife are about to drown, each by themselves, in their stagnated relationship; he further realizes how her personality has been subordinated to his needs, reduced to "a pillow to fall back on." (112) The story formulates this consciousness in preparation for its focal point toward the end, when Villy tries to change the situation. The degree of estrangement between him and his wife has become so severe that it is almost impossible to reverse their longstanding habit of living past each other in individual isolation. Above all, communication has to be re-learned because it only resembles a set of phrases and gestures used automatically and substituted for a genuine exchange of actual personal feelings.

That individual awareness alone does not suffice is emphasized in "The Telephone Call," where disquieting feelings are discussed in time and, as a result, isolation is at least momentarily overcome. To what extent general indifference can be transcended in the private and public spheres remains an unanswered question. "'What is it we talk about when we are in the same room?--Work, children, worries, politics, books, the future.'" (97) Palle's dissatisfaction with the routine contact they have with their friends is countered by his wife Birte's answer, which expresses the conviction that nothing more than this accepted norm for contact can be expected from friends: "'Good grief, isn't that plenty? What is it you want?'" (97) The extent to which their lives have become entrenched in a routine can be seen in Palle's inability to communicate his desire for meaningful contact that involves the other person's confidence in him and goes beyond listening to his judgments on current issues. The burden of this routine appears to justify the various coping tactics that lead to adapting to rather than questioning, such as a superficial existence. The close contact with friends in early adulthood, when problems and confidential feelings were shared, and individual vulnerability less covered up was lost and neglected along with their old friends. Palle's consciousness of a surrounding indifference, submerged under a structured everyday routine, is triggered by the ringing telephone which he does not reach in time; unable to imagine who called so late at night, he can only think of an emergency or a wrong number. Who would care about calling them otherwise at this time?

The motif of indifference among people is linked with the motif of death. Twice the same evening, Palle's confrontation with death underscores the inhuman dimension of a well integrated indifference. When his friend Frans, a life-insurance agent, secretly shows him a number of detailed close-up photographs taken by the police to document the suicide of a soldier, Frans exhibits the ghoulish mentality of the routine consumer: "'They should have been in color, (...) We have some that are much better. A man who strangled his five children while the wife was at work.

The smallest was hardly a year old. They were placed in a row.
That was really something. (...)-this is nothing.'" (90) This action of superficially glossing over a human tragedy with all its
underlying problems is paralleled by the war movie Birte and Palle
go to see that same evening. In the film the individual soldier's
tragic fate and the message of peace are subordinated to the effects of suspense through monumental horror, and the primary interest of the filmmaker in exploiting the documentary material for
commercial purposes becomes evident. Palle's awareness of indifference, haunting despair and individual isolation centers on the
remembered image of the photograph of the soldier who has committed suicide: "'Strange that someone could react so strongly,
take life so seriously as to die of it.' Palle was both shaken
and envious." (90) Palle's envy that someone was able to feel so
intensely marks his own thought process about the general lack of
intense, genuine feelings in his everyday life. Palle's third
confrontation with death, his wife Birte's account of a skiing incident in which she narrowly escaped death, bridges the main
motifs of indifference, isolation, and death. Here Birte confides
the mental anxiety she experienced, and that it was followed by a
renewed appreciation for life and Palle; above all, she admits
that she made the mistake of forgetting that. Her confidential
account restores their genuine communication beyond the erotic
dimension; it is based on Birte's return to herself and on Palle's
realization that it is here in their private realm of their marriage, where genuine communication must begin. He therefore does
not answer the telephone when it finally rings again. Among all
the stories, this ending in "The Telephone Call" constitutes the
most hopeful signal for a possible regeneration of meaningful contact.

     By contrast, in "In the Course of Last Year" ("Det sidste års
tid") the characters do not "talk about things while there is
time." (148) This insight comes too late for the first person narrator; it comes after thirty-eight years and the death of his
severely alienated wife. Her efforts to shock her husband into
communicating with her both verbally and erotically had failed
because his notions of kindness and tact repressed any arising
problems by ignoring them. The resulting mediocrity in their
relationship--where deeper feelings were never shared, not even
anger, where discrepancies were levelled into a bland harmony as
each partner withdrew from the other--culminated in the total
isolation of death. In the husband's retrospective self-
accusation, he links his inability to communicate with the effects
of childhood conditioning. His aversion to family fights, which
caused him to react by withdrawing, was later transferred to his
married life, where avoiding any friction eventually corresponded
to evading all non-routine communication. For our modern Western
civilization, he thus stands as a shocking example of "one-
dimensional man" to use Herbert Marcuse's term.

V   Double Lives

The other three stories placed last in this collection, "The
Pants" ("Bukserne"), "The Passage" ("Passagen"), and the title
story "The Pillows" ("Puderne") all point to a fundamental neglect
that occurred during the protagonist's childhood or youth and contributed to a later double life as a negative hero.   Having only
reacted to their environment, never having acquired a critical,
self-defining independence to their surroundings, these heroes are
trapped with their identity problems and the support strategies
they have generated in order to cope with their everyday ex-
istences;   that means primarily coping with themselves in relation
to other people.
     Through the juxtaposition of childhood and mid-life in "The
Pants," the social environment is depicted as partly responsible
for the lack of self-definition for which the adult character
devises substitutions.   The thematic inter-relation of these two
phases is concentrated in one symbol, the pants. Never allowed to
develop his personal wishes in choosing his clothes and toys
despite vehement protests, the narrator recalls how being forced
to grow up adapting to hand-me-downs from his brother continues to
determine his clothing habits. The fact that he only buys second-
hand clothes illustrates his dependency on the past. To what extent he has been conditioned to adapt and only react instead of
acting autonomously becomes evident through the pair of pants
which--like the other clothes bought second-hand--lend him an
imagined substitute identity. They complement him, provide an additional structure for his life, direct him in his search for
friendship with other people whom their previous owner might have
known. As the incident with this particular pair of pants
reveals, however, his difficulties in life stem not merely from an
undeveloped identity. When the pants lead him to a shabby bar at
the harbor, the disappointment he experiences through their
"directives"--the failure to make a possibly meaningful acquaintance with a woman--exposes his disillusionment with life over the
lack of warmth and caring among people. He experiences a loss of
meaning and hope which leads to a withdrawal that falls short of
suicide. Sensitivity and the habit of merely reacting to an
alienating environment have resulted in a state of passive suffering. His expectation that his life can be given meaning by
what is external to the self, such as women or second-hand
clothes, only blocks his initiative and prevents him from finding
a way to independently shape a fulfilling life. Even if he
decides to act at the moment when they "direct" him into the
water--taking them off and throwing them into the harbor--it is
only a temporary self-assertion. His apprehension when he has to
borrow some pants at the police station in order to get home does
not indicate whether or not he has given up a habit which corresponds to seeking a kind of guardianship.
     In this story, the seriousness of the theme is mitigated by
the first person narrator's tragicomic situation. As he explains
to an officer at the police station why he was running down the
street without pants, his constant associative switching between

the present and his childhood past is determined by his desire to
include the details important to him on the one hand and the
policeman's impatience on the other. The protagonist's account
that he had to throw the pants into the harbor because they were
still pulling him in after he had changed his mind about following
their "directives" covers up his desperation and his suicide attempt through his comic emphasis placed on habits, dislikes, and
procedure in preparation for drowning himself: "But which leg
should go first now? I tried to remember which leg I usually
start with, but that's something you never seriously ascertain,
and when it counts, you just stand there. You simply lack
previous knowledge in that situation. I could also go out
sideways or backwards, or I could lie down and let myself roll
over the edge." (126) Details are expanded and blown up out of
proportion compared to the task he has set himself. Not only does
he perpetuate a confusion which corresponds to the extent of his
despair, he also generates excuses for evading this task thus
revealing that he, in fact, does not want to die. It is a technique Andersen uses to achieve a comic distance from the tragic
aspects of the situation, a technique of defamiliarization well
known from his poetry, and especially evident in "Slug a bed."
    The poem "Goodness" comes to mind when considering the theme
and structure of the story "The Passage" ("Passagen"), where again
the individual, isolated from the warmth of close relationship
with others, seeks to substitute something for it and finds refuge
in a self-made support structure. Lars Hansen, the main
character, deludes himself with the fixation that he can construct
a new life with the trivial objects he collects as a pickpocket
after his routine day at the office. The hope of finding the happiness and warmth of human contact reaches its peak in the excitement when yet another object is secured from someone's pocket.
This hope takes shape in the visionary image of a hand:

> Sometimes I'm possessed by the idea that the ob-
> ject I shall find in the pocket is (...) a hand, a
> real living hand. It doesn't discourage me, yes--
> my heart begins to pound at the thought, but it
> doesn't prevent me from slipping my hand down, on
> the contrary, it might be the best thing that
> could happen, a warm living hand which seizes hold
> of mine--hard and angry it would probably be, but
> nevertheless it would be far better than all those
> cigarette-lighters and pipe-cleaners, all of a
> sudden I would get over the problem of having to
> piece an existence together from all these
> objects.[7]

It is clear that these objects are merely a substitution, but a
highly desperate one, for interpersonal contact and a new life.
By creating an illusion of constant achievement and progress, they
allow Hansen to avoid facing his situation as it really is, for
his tactics actually mean further procrastination in reaching for
the new beginning to which he aspires. Like the speaker in the
poem "Goodness," he is content to remain alone; we are witness to

a grotesque substitution, epitomized as Hansen sucks on one of his objects--a lady's glove filled with red pudding, a replacement for warmth and contact. This glove becomes a metaphor for happiness, referring to both infantility and sexuality. The tripartite structure that can be observed in many poems--desire, actual state, chosen consequence--also applies to the underlying structure of this story. As in most of Andersen's stories, we perceive a stagnant situation without closure corresponding to the protagonist's chosen consequence: "I am happy just now, but shall I be content with that in the long run?--and at the same time I think: in the future I shan't be able to think of eating sago pudding in any other way."[8]

In spite of this somber anticipation of a constantly prolonged and unresolved state of personal isolation, the critic Elias Bredsdorff calls the story "playful and charming."[9] He might have been persuaded to come to this conclusion, which highlights only one side of the story, as a result of the narrative technique Andersen employs. We are not far from a situation which resembles that of an experiment: the central character plays a role in a secluded environment under intense self-observation. Accordingly, details of an often whimsical, peculiar behavior pattern are placed in the center of attention, and all activity related by the stream of consciousness technique takes on the appearance of a game with intricate rules. The charm evoked by naiveté of scheme and innocence in its pursuit may appeal to the reader, but to judge the entire story by these traits is to neglect their relative weight within the narrative technique. Andersen's use of distortions defamiliarizes the charming and gives his scenes an element of the grotesque. After all, Lars Hansen is deeply involved in a search for what may have caused his present state. Parallel to his attempts to break out of his increasingly meaningless existence, he tries to find the missing link between his past happiness and his present dissatisfaction with a life which--up to this critical point--was determined by these very memories of a harmonious and happy childhood:

> The more I dig out, the more I distrust my memory,
> it must be all lies there must be some kind of a
> deception, it can't be this that has made up my
> life, there must be something at the bottom or in
> between that I can't quite get hold of, something
> that can show me why my life has been the way it
> has, why I have ended up in the Passage, so that I
> can see where I've gone wrong and start again.
> All the rest I cheerfully remember must be an act,
> a performance which is to keep me outside as an
> observer; I can applaud or criticize, but the play
> is over, it has come to an end without my being
> able to do anything about it.[10]

Hansen's protest against a hidden, built-in mistake in his life runs parallel to the desire for a re-integration into lost happiness; he is, however, not able to realize that it is the concept itself he needs to revise, and that this revision cannot be

restricted to his life alone but must be extended to the normative
values of his cultural environment. Consequently, he finds himself caught between a social pressure to conform and an individual
pressure to rebel, feels kept "outside," having had no influence
on forming the idea of what a happy and meaningful life ought to
be like. The untranslatable ambiguity of the Danish word for performance, "forestilling," which also means idea or concept, points
to the underlying conceptual problem in the life of Hansen and can
be extended to Andersen's heroes in other stories.

Hansen's situation parallels that of Roquentin in Sartre's
Nausea before Roquentin's revelation about his existence. Each of
them senses the presence of a vague, forgotten problem from the
past which makes itself felt in his present life through the intense awareness of a profound emptiness. In addition, each of
them is panic-stricken when, in sudden moments, he feels his control over the objects around him slipping away,[11] in Hansen's case
when he fears being trapped by and in his clothes. But Hansen is
portrayed at a stage which Roquentin is leaving. Hansen, after
all, is still trying to improve his situation by seeking adventures in the passage at night waiting for the great event which
could change his life at any time--although the chances for such a
salvation diminishes the more he settles into his world of substitutions.

The stage of hidden protest illustrates how social conditioning and the protagonist's semi-conscious aversion to its effects have led to a schizophrenic attitude, for coping with daily
life would otherwise be impossible. It is reminiscent of Brecht's
similar treatment of daily coping in The Good Woman of Sezuan. Unlike Brecht, however, Andersen often includes pathological features to stress the degree of individual estrangement. The hero's
double life--one public in an average routine and one private
bordering on, if not actually involving, criminal activity--is
depicted graphically in "The Passage" and in the title story "The
Pillows." Like many of Andersen's heroes, the restless
protagonists in these two stories are propelled by social pressure
and by an inner pressure of their own as they witness a split
within themselves and their world. Whether the protagonist experiences a lack of meaningful personal contact or downright abuse
by others, usually superiors, he resorts to extreme measures for
coping with his situation. In order to preserve his job performance and emotional balance when interacting with others on a
daily basis, he channels his frustration or aggression into an
unusual behavior pattern in the privacy of the dark and of his own
room. While in "The Passage" he had turned into a pickpocket to
compensate for a lack of personal contact, his strategy in "The
Pillows" marks a peak of seriousness.

On a daily basis, the protagonist of "The Pillows" blends in
well with his social environment and projects the image of a
friendly, easy-going, and successful small businessman with an
average family. But all his life, he has maintained his well-
adjusted behavior by secretly making dolls from pillows and
stuffed burlap sacks to represent his daily tormentors: the
bigger boys who beat him up in the schoolyard, the girlfriend who
left him for another man, the sergeant who urinated into his soft

drink because he refused to drink beer--these dolls are in turn
subjected to sadistic torture. While he stresses that he is no
Nazi, his secret ways of retaliating for the fears, insults, and
aggressions he suffers do expose Fascist tendencies in everyday
life, because his tactics are often patterned after his experiences. But such coping techniques do not assist in
eliminating the problem; instead, they serve to internalize and
reinforce suffering, aggression, and self-pity, no matter how
vehemently they underscore the gesture of protest. This protest
remains a private protest; the protagonist remains imprisoned in
his own strategy, becomes dependent on it and addicted to it. His
coping evades the basic problem of defending his code of ethics
against his aggressors because of a myopic concentration on self-
protection whose only function it is to preserve the surface appearance of a balanced personality. The danger of such escapism
is demonstrated through the eventual collapse of the hero as a
well-functioning citizen. Although his protective strategy
clearly has arisen from the protest against an inhuman environment
where the weaker or non-conforming person is in a difficult position, the solution of harmony it is aimed at reveals the influence
of the superficial values offered by society to cover up and thus
integrate problems. This defeat of genuine protest points to a
stunted growth, thematically depicted by the protagonist's
systematic repression of one side of his individuality. His
clinging to a concept of normality amounts to an act of violence
against himself and illustrates well a side of what R. D. Laing
termed "our present pervasive madness that we call normality,
sanity, freedom."[12]
     The failure of the protagonist to take the risk of developing
his own identity demonstrates how life as a result has been built
on substitutions symbolized by the pillows. Since these pillows
assist in the acquisition of a mere social identity, they only
provide the illusion of control representing for the protagonist
his mastering of past problems. Consequently, this kind of self-
deception, which Ibsen refers to as the lie we live by, constitutes his vulnerability. After having disposed of the old pillows at his wife's request, he is left defenseless and is
gradually overpowered by his unresolved past and the competitive
techniques of the new supermarket's manager. With the concrete
images of his former control gone, he has lost his orientation and
is haunted by his past mistakes in the shape of pillows everywhere. The difficulties of life he has neglected to face in the
past now confront him relentlessly. Andersen's depiction of this
situation brings to mind the recent reformulation of an age-old
theme by the Mexican writer Carlos Fuentes that the ghosts of the
past, when thrown out the window, come back in some day through
the front door wearing strange disguises.[13] The universal human
challenge to take a stand in time as stated here is presented in
Andersen's story "The Pillows" by focusing on the individual as
the guilty victim who suddenly one day is confronted with "the
other reality," that is, the reality he has repressed.
     Here as in other stories communication is a key motif, and
direct communication has been replaced by evasive techniques.
Communication with others has been relegated to the protagonist's

one-dimensional thrashing-it-out in self-seclusion with the pillows whenever this was the way of least resistance, while communication that would disturb the semblance of harmony and courtesy was avoided. Thus the defensive stance, once developed to
obtain the illusion of acting--that one-way communication--becomes
an attitude toward life. In a Surrealistic scene at the culmina-
tion of the story, it is the direct and honest exchange with his
wife, which he has neglected in daily life, that demonstrates the
vital necessity of sharing thoughts and feelings, including anger
and self-pity; mutual support must counterbalance external pressures before they lead to violence as symbolized by the Surrealistic destruction of the supermarket on part of the narrator
and his pillow allies. Likewise, communication determines the
story's stream of consciousness, because the motivating force for
the narrator's recollection is to some day tell his children "the
whole thing in a language they can understand."[14] Throughout his
retrospective account, the motif of communication thus signifies
the hero's deficient awareness of his personal situation. Although he warns of the danger of waking up "in the wrong place"
some day, he does not trace this danger to the basic mistake he
made: that all he developed was a defensive shell instead of the
relative personal autonomy obtained through an assertive ethical
stance. Seeking refuge in a fixed support structure is thereby
dramatically exposed as a strategy that is detrimental for the
personality, if not self-destructive. Symbolically, this is expressed through the hero's double life as it comes to a climax in
the Surrealistic division of his personality when he reaches a
state of partial awareness and insanity.

The fact that the negative hero chooses a persona instead of
a personality is given symbolic significance by a complete division in "A Happy Person" ("Et lykkeligt menneske"), the last story
in Andersen's second collection of short fiction,
Fats Olsen and Other Stories. With this allegorical story, he
demonstrates how fundamental individual problems are covered up by
daily wearing a mask. Christiansen, the happy man in the center
of this story, hides his aggressions, dislikes, and bad humor so
he can always appear understanding and agreeable for he cannot
identify with his petty characteristics. He conforms to the concept of harmony and happiness, whose trade-mark, a never ending
broad smile, is already satirized earlier in the poem "Smile." Accordingly, he lives in agony like many other heroes in Andersen's
stories, in this case always watchful in order not to reveal himself to his family and friends: "I am sitting on needles, walking
on hot coals, sleeping on a bed of nails."[15] To avoid collapsing
under this burden, he takes off alone for the family's summer cottage to live out his aggressions, drop his smile altogether, and
tyrannize the people he meets. Besides relieving his constant
inner pressure in this way, he also has to bear, along with a fear
of discovery, his feelings of guilt for spreading happiness in his
family without deserving to be praised for it. This changes
during one of his trips to the cottage when he makes a genuine effort to defeat the unacceptable part of himself in the encounter
with Mr. Pedersen, who personifies all the petty and aggressive
characteristics of Christiansen and can be considered the hero's

undesirable side. Pedersen seems to have come to the lake for the same purpose as Christiansen, and soon they are both preoccupied with antagonizing each other. Their encounter develops into a fight for life in a boat out on the lake. It amounts to an allegorical fight between Christiansen and the negative side of his personality in which he can only save himself by swimming to the shore, because the unbearable thought that his evil counterpart might defeat him inspires him with unusual strength. Although now for the first time he feels he has earned his happiness--the admiration and respect he receives at home--it is clear that no permanent change has taken place. Pedersen may also have swum to safety and may run into him again in town. While Christiansen, the first person narrator, justifies his living between extremes by stressing the positive ideals he is motivated by, he cannot conceal the fact that he evades balancing the rigidly opposing forces in his personality: the one he wants to be with the one he is. Driven by the underlying fear of risking his happiness, he reveals a narrowly defined concept of true happiness. Harmony at the cost of coming to terms with his personality and admitting his weaknesses leaves him dependent on his substitute strategy. It amounts to a state of existing outside himself for Christiansen.

VI The Daily Game

A thematic expansion marks a number of stories in Andersen's second volume Fats Olsen and Other Stories. Here, the rules and standards governing everyday existence, and thereby the strategies of the protagonists, reveal a Darwinistic social climate that centers on the survival of the fittest, or more precisely, on the self-assertion of the strongest, and that means primarily the shrewdest. Coping with daily existence clearly requires an understanding of the often ruthless treatment the individual is subjected to, as summed up in "The Bouncer" ("Udsmideren") with the almost proverbial wisdom: "No one is indispensable." (29) Although one can hardly object to this basic fact, it is quite another matter to build on it by treating people as if they were merchandise. Against such an attitude based essentially on marketing principles, Jensen, the bouncer, protests when he realizes how it affects him. His counter-statement, "But you are damned indispensable to yourself," (29) touches the core of the problem in Andersen's stories. At stake is the individual's psychological self-preservation, the pursuit of a meaningful and happy life. Accordingly, Jensen leaves no doubt about what his job means to him; it is responsible for a turn in his life from a barroom brawler to the bouncer and respected doorman of a dance restaurant:

> The first year was simply the best time of my
> life. I quickly figured out the worst types, and
> out of the way they went. Only rarely did I now
> have to hit anybody. I now had a blue uniform

with a red collar, white gloves and a cap. (...)
In a year's time, it became--thanks to me--a place
where nice and peaceful people could come and enjoy themselves; the sale of sandwiches, liquor and
coffee increased.
(26)

The sense of self-respect and personal value he derives from this
additional evening job, which he got by accident after a fight,
has brought about a meaningful change in his life that should not
be confused with vanity. It has given him the opportunity to be
in contact with people without having to fight for it, without
having to gain respect through fistfights, and above all it has
provided him with the strong possibility to establish a meaningful
relationship with Gerda, the young woman in the cloakroom.
    Contrasted with this development is the strictly profit-
oriented attitude of the restaurant's owners. Once the establishment has become respectable, the owner sells it for a good price
to a former waiter of Divan II, a restaurant in Copenhagen's
amusement park Tivoli. From this new owner's interest in maximum
profit, danger arises for Jensen's newly acquired position, since
he has made himself superfluous from a business perspective.   His
rebellion against the reductive and utilitarian standards that
threaten his position is paralleled by his insight that he must
cope with tacitly accepted rules of a strictly business nature.
No matter how dispensable he may be according to those rules,   he
has to prevent his reverting to his former existence. His preven-
tive measures consist of playing the very game against which his
protest is directed: each evening, he selects a few visitors who
lend themselves to being thrown out or not admitted, thus proving
how indispensable he is for the continued profitability of the
establishment.
    This defensive position also determines the   narrative
framework of the story: "I'm no brawler, not anymore," the
story's opening sentence, is complemented by the final sentences:
"I'm not at all out to fight; that was in the old days. But I
don't put up with just anything. That's simply the way I am.
People just have to take me as I am, or else it's out with you.
Cheers." (32) Jensen projects a strong sense of being justified in
his action, because he has led up to his shrewd solution by constantly stressing that he is a man of integrity even if his
behavior may suggest the opposite. With a careful balancing act
between past and present, his focus alternates constantly between
his need for a happy life and the obstacles he has experienced.
This need is depicted indirectly by Jensen's emphasis as narrator
on the brutal environment of his childhood.

And the way my father treated my mother, you just
can't imagine it.   One time, she came home with
most of her teeth in a bloody handkerchief because
the old man thought she had stared a bit too much
at another guy. That time, I was unfortunately a
little too small to do anything about it, but if
it happened today...Well, now he has kicked the
bucket, thank God.   (22)

Having grown up with the experience of not only violence toward the weaker but also of his own powerlessness and anger in view of such immoral and brutal conduct, Jensen explains his later reputation as a barroom brawler by pointing out his moral reasons for getting involved in fights: "All this business here of giving ladies black and blue marks gives me finger cramps, you know, and I just can't straighten them again before the skunk is on the floor and calls for his old mom." (22) When justifying himself and his behavior, Jensen is building his account on a number of either openly or tacitly accepted norms in society. Morally, he appears as the fair and righteously angry advocate of the weaker; likewise, he appears justified in his tactics toward the restaurant's new owner because he is treated unfairly by being considered superfluous although he had actually made the place respectable. And finally, the inhuman aspect of a solely utilitarian approach to business, exchanging people like objects, calls for siding with him in protest. After the clever presentation of his case, he can count on general acclaim as the little man who has outwitted the profit monger, and he has secured Gerda's admiration in any case. But is he really as fair and humane as he projects himself to be when he picks on a prospective guest, refusing him entry on the grounds of being obviously drunk because he had stumbled over the unfamiliar threshold? Jensen's shrewdness as a narrator is surely necessary, since he retaliates at the cost of an uninvolved person, adapting to the utilitarian principles of the game he had reacted against. The fact that he sees no other solution but to acknowledge the widely accepted norms and use them for his self-protection suggests a continuing feeling of powerlessness as far as the general system is concerned. Only within a limited sphere can he prove to be the stronger, at least temporarily. Like Fats Olsen, he is engaged in the act of balancing his ethics with his survival tactics. Although Jensen does not have to fear any physical danger and actually succeeds with his strategy, he cannot be considered the positive figure he might appear to be; after all, he integrates himself and thus confirms the system's strength despite his feeling that something is wrong. But Jensen only associates the problems he experiences with those who have confronted him as opponents of his ethics or vital interests--his father, bullies in the bars, or the restaurant's owner--yet he does not perceive the flaws in the accepted value system; he merely reacts to these flaws.

In the story "It Must Be Possible (or: A Day in the Botanical Gardens)" ("Det må kunne lade sig gøre (eller: En dag i Botanisk have)"), a "lonely man"--the typical protagonist in Andersen's stories--is also characterized as having very well internalized certain values he grew up with. With the ironic distance of a third person narrator's omniscient perspective, Andersen depicts here the narrowing effect society's directives have on the individual personality:

> He is considered, and likes to be considered, a
> nice but somewhat colorless guy who takes care of
> himself; and due to an alloy of secret pride and

> modesty, he would never beg a person for contact--
> would not turn his back on it either but rather
> his side.   (10)

He has learned his lessons well, evades contact and all the risks
connected with getting involved. Making every effort to blend into his environment, in appearance and behavior, he adapts to the
rules he must live by, restricting his personality with a
grotesque mixture of obedience and self-protection. By persuading
himself that he does not want what he does not have, he guards
himself against the emotional necessities of life. Since no pets
are allowed where he lives, "he does not walk around dreaming
about something unattainable" but instead looks indifferent, if
not the other way, whenever he sees a nice dog, always feeling
supported by existing social norms. His meeting with the squirrels in the Botanical gardens, however, reveals his longing for
contact and his joy over the unexpected interest they take in him,
even if it is only an interest in food. His tragicomic pedantry
in trying to feed the squirrels while being overwhelmed by
pigeons, attests to his great isolation, to his inexperience in
taking the risk of making contact. It also satirizes the restric-
tive rules with which society has filled our daily lives. Part of
him self-consciously expects to encounter regulations for his conduct everywhere; another part of him ironically expresses its
astonishment about their surprising absence:

> How loudly is it actually allowed to hiss at pid-
> geons?   There ought to be a notice about that in
> the garden. A hissing-regulation. (...) Is it
> permitted to push pidgeons? There ought to be a
> pushing-regulation too. Surely, it is not per-
> mitted to kick pidgeons, but it would be totally
> wrong to call this a kick. Push covers it much
> better.
> (11-12)

It is precisely here that Andersen's social criticism is lodged by
alluding to society's abundance of restricting directives. The
lonely man in this story has thoroughly unlearned spontaneity and
initiative.   Instead, he has developed a dependency on rules as a
secure structure for his life. When he finally dares to make contact with the squirrel, he has to face the difficulties of
reaching out: his peanuts are not wanted; he should have bought
hazelnuts or almonds. Yet the story's didactic mode is clear.
What follows is not another withdrawal parallel to an earlier
rejection he experienced by a girlfriend as a young adult; instead, the symbolic scene in the park underscores the necessity
that he must keep on trying. He must take the initiative and
thereby the risk of establishing contact with others.   At the
story's end, it has become an imperative that he overcome those
rules which only cause a meaningless restriction of his personality.   Also, through his symbolic occupation as waiter he has
the opportunity to expand his role from simply taking orders to
actually reaching out. "Life is not easy. But on the other hand,

you should keep life off your back." (19) His wavering between withdrawal and meaningful involvement is resolved in favor of the latter when the lonely man's insight into the importance, joy, and possibility of interpersonal contact suggests to him that his own good mood might be vital for an improved relationship with his customers. The story, besides criticizing society's functional aspects, emphasizes individual responsibility for creating a more humane social environment. It reiterates the challenge expressed in "The Break-Up" at the beginning of Andersen's first collection of short stories and points to the dialectical pattern of his main theme: individual stagnation must be overcome in a process of personal development.

That this challenge cannot be substituted for, not even with the ideal of democratic principles, is demonstrated in Andersen's focus on marriage in "Ulla and Søren (or: Housewarming)" ("Ulla og Søren (eller: Housewarming)"). Here the third person narrator presents an analysis in the style of a report about this attempted model democracy between two and exposes an intricate psychological game based on an ideal turned into an absolute norm: that no one partner should dominate the other in important decisions. For practical daily application, this means they never get their way. In order to achieve a compromise as close as possible to what they each had originally wanted, both Ulla and Søren have to play a strategically planned role in their discussions of significant plans. While this marriage overtly resembles a harmonious state, it is governed in every sphere by a fixed set of rules and thus amounts to a constant power struggle for the sake of principles and at the cost of spontaneity. Consequently, this psychological tight rope they walk on snaps when Søren behaves out of order and spontaneously explains to their son that they will have a party after moving into their new house: "Such a new house can easily feel a little cold in the beginning, kind of a little strange; it has to be warmed up so it will be nice to live in, and that you do by inviting all the people you know." (124) For once, he states openly what he wants, supported enthusiastically by their son, but only to encounter Ulla's opposition, with the result that the party is not given and the new house never gets warm for him; their balance can never be restored and eventually results in their divorce.

Rejecting short-sighted tactics for daily coping, Andersen thus places a distinct focus on the individual's need for developing as genuine an identity as possible. This theme is played through in many variants, for it comprises a never-ending challenge for the protagonist in most stories of Andersen's two collections. The challenging task for the heroes in these stories is how to be part of a group and still be themselves, starting from the smallest unit of two in a marriage or friendship to larger groups of friends, colleagues, or neighbors. In their Kafkaesque struggles, their sometimes manic or phobic behavior can be considered a gesture of despair reminiscent of Dostoevsky's underground man, who exclaims to his readers that he, in contrast to most people, dares to be crazy.[16] Like a number of Andersen's heroes, he lives his traumas fully.

Similarly, the demonic traits of some of Andersen's "small men" can be understood as signs of their fear, their "dread of the good," since they are depicted as living in a state of angst, analogous to the one defined by Kierkegaard as "demoniacal," that is, as "an unfree relation to the good."[17] Existing in the bonds of fear has become a way of life for them, not only because they chose a system of artificial support but also because they have accomodated themselves to it and thus have become rooted in their state of bondage. Their fear is often made concrete by means of objects which fail to work as planned; this reification of angst is enlarged in the short parabolical story "The Shoes" ("Skoene"), which revolves around the narrator's panic that all of a sudden his shoes--that is, his way of life--may no longer fit and thus threaten his daily existence. It must be stressed, however, that daring to be crazy only conveys part of the problem. To those who are so firmly entrenched in a system of fixed habits, routines, and seemingly unchangeable laws that they do not question it, the deviant behavior of these "small men" appears to be crazy. But the basic conflict symbolized in these stories, as in a great number of Andersen's poems, runs parallel to the one formulated by Sartre in his novel Nausea, and it is with Sartre's main character, Antoine Roquentin, that a protest must be raised against labeling as "crackpots" those who have become conscious of an essential emptiness in their lives and in their surroundings and, as a result, no longer fit into the standard patterns of behavior.

Although Andersen's portraits often evoke sympathy for his characters because of their naiveté, helplessness, and good will, their counter-productive coping techniques and the social norms they conform to are critically exposed as contributing to an in-human environment. Andersen's emphasis on the dialectical process between the individual and society, a process that calls for a genuine effort to resolve confrontations, does not allow us to classify his stories simply as " a reader's cabaret." Instead of a rigid critical opposition to society, Andersen seeks to demonstrate mutual responsibilities and mistakes by means of his fictional parables. Through the behavior of his negative heroes and their self-deluding choices for a fulfilling life, Andersen exposes the basic error of choosing a blind pursuit of being[18] behind the individual's daily struggle for meaning. In a sense, these literary efforts can be compared to the task R. D. Laing had set himself when, in the framework of existential phenomenology, he decided "to articulate what the other's 'world' is and his way of being in it."[19]

7

The Narrator in Fear of Discovery: The Case of "Fats Olsen"

Benny Andersen is well known for his portrayals of strange, often tragicomic characters whose behavior deviates from the socially accepted norm. Although critics have had a tendency to stress the humorous aspects of these outsider figures along with the visible social criticism, Andersen's image should not be restricted to that of the amusing advocate of the underdog in a modern, impersonal society. He should certainly be read--as the Swedish critic Lars Grahn has argued--wherever the petit-bourgeois power struggles take place, since Andersen exposes how thinly a facade of so-called civilized behavior covers up potential violence.[1] But while Andersen takes a strong critical stance toward a hostile social environment, he not only depicts the daily struggle of his characters sympathetically, but also subjects them to criticism, for instance through the narrator's clever manipulations. Because of the narrative focus, this twofold purpose may easily be overlooked in some cases, as in "Fats Olsen" the title story of Andersen's second collection of short stories.

The shopkeeper Olsen presents to us a social model of armed neutrality from his small Danish community, in which he is the potential target for violence. His uneasy feeling that the parents in his neighborhood do not trust him, because he lives alone, and therefore suspect him of being a potential child molester has proven to be correct. Olsen's shop has been ransacked by a mob of angry fathers after he has been accused of molesting his neighbor's little daughter, Nina Thorkildsen, when he actually has saved her from falling into a pond in the forest.

Although Nina and her mother have cleared him of the accusation,
Olsen knows that the suspicion will continue to exist.   While
Olsen, the first person narrator of the story, gives his account
of these events, his deliberations as to whether or not he should
stay in town focus on his difficulties in living with the unjustly
imposed role as social outsider. Well equipped for this role, he
is the ugly duckling who remains exactly that both physically and
in a moral sense. His snub snout stems from a fist fight in his
sailor days caused by his twitchy eye, with which he was thought
to have winked at another sailor's girl. In addition, Olsen is
overweight, unmarried, and teased by the children of the neighborhood, who invade his garden to raid his apple tree. All this adds
up to give him the appearance of a morally suspect loner in the
eyes of his neighbors. Some readers may find it difficult to accept this image painted by Olsen's account, may consider it to be
exaggerated; others may feel compassion for him, and still others
will see in him a clever victim. The analysis will argue in support of the last position and will center on Olsen's strategic
function as a first person narrator in order to provide a key to
the complexity of his personal situation.

     The exposed problem area is a familiar one: the friction
between the private and public spheres. Although Olsen's conflict
is not unusual, his strategy of self-protection is--both in his
actions as a member of society and as a narrator advocating his
case. What he terms "this sociologically interesting process"
raises questions about the quality of the social environment we
have created, about the norms we follow and the values we adhere
to.   Since his own precarious situation is central to such questions, Olsen attempts to stimulate an awareness of his difficulties and their context. But this requires a cautious, indirect
approach to his reader, who might otherwise shrug off the problem
as exaggerated, or even side with the "normal" people in the community, and perhaps discover a flaw in Olsen's self-protective
strategy.   Olsen therefore prepares us to see the events from his
perspective, and at first, we wonder why he places so much emphasis on justifying his decision to fell his apple tree. Only
gradually does he disclose its role as he provides details about
the hostility he has encountered, leading up to the story's
climax, the ransacking of his shop. Already from the story's very
first paragraph, he lays the foundation for his lengthy apologia
and establishes a partnership with the reader in what appears to
be a soliloquy:

          I'll probably have to cut down that apple tree.
          It's really too bad--it's such a nice tree, bears
          good fruit too, Cox Orange, not too large, concen-
          trated savor and juicy through and through. But
          things can't go on like this. Or else I'll have
          to   move--sell the tobacco shop, give up my
          editorial work, and move. Not on your life.   It
          would just be the same thing all over again in a
          new place. And abandon the paper?   Never.   Who
          would edit it then? None of the nitwits around
          here wants to write anything but soccer betting

> slips.   And who but me wants to spend most of his
> leisure time working at an unpaid job?   No, if I
> drop out, it'll just turn into an advertising
> sheet again.   No, it'll have to be the apple tree
> that goes.   Poor, unsuspecting apple tree.(33)[2]

While he retains his cover, defending his decision to fell the
apple tree because the parents seem to consider it the "bait" he
uses to lure the children into his garden, Olsen carefully approaches us with the theme of group prejudice.   But before we know
anything about the discrimination against him, we have already
been given a primarily negative character sketch of the local
people: not only do they exclude Olsen when it comes to being
friendly but they also are nitwits, not interested in anything but
soccer and cars, too indolent to bother with thinking about
problematic issues,   and above all they are against anyone who is
different.   Contrasted with them is Olsen, the laudable exception.
In his newspaper articles based on the intelligent perception of
his social situation, he assumes the role of community pedagogue;
here, by his indirect attempts to make people conscious of their
lynch mentality, he proves that he is thinking, and in his carefully balanced daily interaction with people he demonstrates the
application of his psychological insight, following a strategy according to the motto: "As long as they didn't know where they had
me, I could sleep in peace." (44)
     Olsen realizes that in view of the   narrow-mindedness around
him he poses a threat to the neighboring families, particularly
since his shop and garden provide ample opportunity for him to
meet and interact with their children.   He also seems to know how
fear of a threat increases with the uncertainty about it.   For
this reason, he exhibits his innocence by keeping open the back
room to his shop and by remaining in the visual range of the
neighbors on his walks by the forest.   Although it is clear to him
that he can neither change their opinion nor curb their imagina-
tions, Olsen makes these concessions to his neighbors and claims
to understand their protectiveness:

> And the funny thing is that I can well understand
> the parent's attitude.   It is absolutely clear to
> me that Thorkildsen has to be the way he is toward
> me, I would probably react just like him if I had
> children. (45)

He even goes so far as to concede that the parents, for example
little Nina Thorkildsen's father, act reasonably, for he himself
might be equally protective as a father, thus assuring us of his
credibility as a fair narrator.   By virtue of his special position, Olsen has acquired an expanded perspective; yet he transmits
his insight only indirectly through the subtle hints in his
newspaper editorials.   He does not take any initiative in this
regard.   It does not seem to occur to him that he might alleviate
the threat he poses and the resulting suspicion by associating
with his neighbors and allowing them to acquaint themselves with
Olsen the private citizen.   Or is Olsen rejecting this idea for

some untold reason? He must be aware of his neglect, must be
withholding the information of never having tried to come into
closer contact with the other men, for he tries to divert our attention by assuring us that he is no misanthropist:

> I prefer to live alone and take care of myself but
> am neither a hermit nor misanthropic; I devote at
> least as much time to the world around me as to
> myself, it's about fifty-fifty. Both in the shop
> and through work- ing with the newspaper, I satis-
> fy my need to associate with others. (39)

Olsen confuses two issues: the interest in his surroundings, and
the interest in cultivating human relationships beyond the shopkeeper's duty and the editor's allotment of pedagogical argumentation. For him they are identical. By justifying his right to
choose his way of life, Olsen narrows down his focus and conceals
the fact that he has also chosen to isolate himself in his private
sphere. The concessions Olsen makes are designed to ensure his
self-contained life-style but not to reach out, even to a limited
extent, to the people in his neighborhood. He keeps the counter
of his shop and the abstract level of the printed page between
himself and others when he communicates with them: he does not
seek the other men's company.
    Why then has Olsen opened himself to suspicion by choosing
such a reclusive existence? Why doesn't he associate with the
neighbors? Because he has a negative opinion of them and fears to
be rejected if he tried? While he withholds such information from
us, he tells us rather than one of them why he is living alone; by
thus communicating to us his weightiest proof that he lost both
his wife and daughter in his first year of marriage and along with
it the courage to remarry, he conveys the evidence of his "normality" to us only. Perhaps pride or principle require that acceptance of him by his neighbors not be contingent upon the
revelation of his "normal" past. That would be understandable but
it would not exclude a choice of associating with his neighbors,
permitting them to get to know him beyond his roles as shopkeeper
and editor. Instead, however, Olsen promotes the image of an
enemy of the people and, in a manner similar to Ibsen's Dr. Stock-
mann, appears to delude himself in the notion of being stronger in
his isolation than the majority. Although Olsen consciously works
for a strong position based on keeping his neighbors uncertain
about his personality, he does not seem to realize how he actually
augments their insecurity. Are we to believe this of Olsen, the
clever realist? That Olsen has ruled out the strategy of private
contact would be a more plausible conclusion. Even if he impresses on us his complete satisfaction with the extent of human
contact he has through his work, he contradicts himself when he
reveals his longing for the affectionate contact a grand-father
enjoys with his grandchildren. The confidence of Nina Thorkildsen, the neighbor's little daughter, grants him for a moment the
happiness of such a role when he saves her from falling into the
forest pond; at the same time, he knows he will be suspected of
having followed her for a criminal reason.

Could it then be that Olsen rules out closer contact with the other men and families because he has too little in common with them, dislikes to talk only about sports and cars? The interested response and inquiry of Thorkildsen, Nina's father, after Olsen's editorial about the lynch mentality indicates a much less restricted range of interests than Olsen presumed. Could it then be a form of masochism which leads Olsen to select his dangerous strategy or does the suspense of playing a challenging game with high stakes appeal to him? The latter is suggested by his treatment of Thorkildsen when he applies his strategy to him in an attempt to prevent Nina's father from believing that he is luring children into his garden. With this objective in mind, he complains about Nina's participation in the children's apple raid, but rather than dissipating Thorkildsen's insecurity, he actually increases it by a seemingly harmless power match:

> We stared into each other's eyes. The time I was
> a sailor, I became sharp at poker, worked up a
> technique of avoiding to blink for up to a minute.
> Often a blink could be decisive. No, so long as
> we just played this game I wasn't nervous--here I
> knew I was superior to the other stay-at-homes,
> and now it even amused me to play for high stakes.
> 'Perhaps you would have me cut down my tree to get
> some peace from the youngsters?' Thorkildsen
> blinked for the first time. I hadn't yet blinked,
> and I could easily manage at least twenty seconds
> more. (...) Thorkildsen blinked again and lost--
> this game in any case. He picked up his change
> and walked toward the door. 'I'll speak to Nina.'
> I couldn't resist follow- ing up my success and
> making him still more insecure: 'But don't be too
> harsh with her now--I just think that she is far
> too sweet a girl to let herself be enticed to
> anything by the big louts.' He turned in the
> door- way and looked at me for a moment. It was,
> to put it mildly, a grudging glance, but at the
> same time confused. I rubbed my hands when he was
> gone. (43-44)

This key scene provides clues for Olsen's faulty strategy and foreshadows a parallel but reversed scene at the end of the story. Olsen's predicament becomes obvious here: his defensive situation contains the possibility for an offensive move because he feels superior at this game. In analogy to the tension of a high-stakes poker game, Olsen does not show his cards, which is characteristic for his strategy. But the potential for a dangerous turn is already implied by Olsen's getting carried away, enjoying his superiority and his momentary power. He is pushing his luck, venturing out too far in his precarious balancing act. Despite his awareness that he is superior only this very moment but not concerning his overall situation, he plays with Thorkildsen even to the point of using dangerously ambiguous language: "she is far too sweet a girl to let herself be enticed to anything by the big

louts." Of course he is only showing a natural reaction,
delighting in a game he can win--a rare opportunity for him. But
for Olsen, who is painfully aware of his precarious position, it
is essential not to alienate Thorkildsen to the point of confusion
where a threat is likely to emanate.

Thorkildsen's sense that he is deliberately being disoriented
is even more acute in the forest scene later in the story. In
this confrontation, when Olsen has all the odds and a majority of
suspicious fathers against him, he tries a similar technique of
daring his opponents, this time entirely on the verbal level,
which only serves to increase the mob atmosphere. In this
degrading confrontation in the forest, Olsen has to face the men's
readiness to harm him physically because of their unverified assumption that he has molested Nina. Olsen tries to preserve his
dignity and self-esteem by pretending he does not understand what
they assume. Instead of a meek Olsen, the respected shopkeeper
speaks, reminding them of their outstanding accounts and
criticizing them for neglecting their children over their
preference for washing cars or chatting on the telephone. When he
refers to the situation at hand, he reveals in spite of his question that he knows exactly what they are thinking, yet he refuses
to give an explanation they would not believe in any case:

> What did you actually expect, anyway, I said, and
> I believe I spoke rather loudly now. Did you ex-
> pect I would fall down on my knees or that I would
> try to take off or that I would say: I'll cross
> out all your credit if only you'll let me get
> away. If that's what you had expected, you'll
> come to wait out your time.
> (58)

At this point, Olsen cannot back out but has to maintain a strong
defiant position in order to preserve his dignity. At the same
time, he is pushing the tense atmosphere to the point of violent
eruption because his words reflect, besides aggressiveness, a common basis of communication: his presumed guilt. He reveals his
awareness of their tacit assumption when he implies the question:
did you expect me to ask for mercy and make a deal with you by
cancelling your debts and thus acknowledging my guilt? That this
assumption may be false becomes secondary; the mounting tension on
both sides demands a release, which is finally reached in the ransacking of Olsen's shop.

Here, Olsen has become the hunted, and he knew it as he was
sliding into that role. With a touch of gallows humor--drawing on
the analogy of the "big bad wolf" following little Red Riding Hood
before getting caught--he proves that he was right in his negative
assessment of his neighbors, which in turn seems to prove his
theories about their dangerous intolerance and to justify his
feelings of superiority. To be precise, however, the incident
only proves one half of this theories. What it does not prove is
the accuracy of his strategy, for it is evident here that Olsen's
flaw becomes self-perpetuating: since his neighbors had no chance
of getting to know him, yet can sense his deliberate attempt at

disorienting them and his awareness of their suspicion toward him,
they feel justified in their assumption. In addition, Olsen's aggressive behavior encourages their spontaneous, irrational reaction, their desire for violent revenge. Thus Olsen has clearly
underestimated the complexity of social communication. He also
underestimates us, his readers, when he tries to convince us of
the existential necessity for his actions, including his didactic
editorials. But the real motivation for enduring in his situation
can already be detected in the first paragraph of this story:
Olsen's feeling of superiority, his pride of being editor, of
having expanded the local paper to include his enlightening articles. Since these editorials arise out of the tension between
him and the community, he has to preserve that state of tension to
gain satisfaction and self-esteem from his pedagogical role.   Although these articles did not prevent violence, Olsen continues to
believe in their didactic value. By making it a moral issue to
hold out in his difficult balancing act, he convinces himself and
suggests to us how indispensable his editorial contributions are:
"Give up my editorial work and move (?) (...) And desert the
paper? Never." Especially by choosing an emotionally charged word
like abandon, he implies that it is his moral duty to stay, and he
further supports this view by pointing out the virtues of using
his head and donating most of his spare time to unpaid work for
the paper in contrast to the "nitwits" in town.

   Olsen is thus forced to develop a strategy of tight rope
balancing both for living and for narrating. The incidents with
Nina in the garden and in the forest jeopardize both, for Nina,
the only innocent and humane figure in Olsen's account, is also
the unpredictable element posing a threat to his strategy of scare
tactics toward the children when they raid his apple tree. She is
not afraid of him, she even has confidence in him later when he
helps her find her way out of the forest. Nina thus exposes
Olsen's soft side and reminds him of the kind of person he would
like to but cannot be because of society's discrimination of him
and because of his misconceived strategy.

   Even though Olsen feels that he has no choice and must withdraw into a self-contained world while playing his dangerous game
of pretending he dislikes children, we should not be persuaded to
think that he is using the right approach. Of course Olsen is no
child molester but a victim of group prejudice; as a narrator,
however, he is unreliable because he has convinced himself of
reacting properly. We can side with him in his opposition to
prejudice, but we must also recognize his own prejudice as it is
revealed in his self-righteous pride. In the negative assessment
of his neighbors, Olsen does not include their unwillingness to
associate with him socially, and he himself assumes it is futile
to even try.   Because he has settled down in his role as social
outsider, he is now forced to fell his apple tree in order to keep
the children away and avert further danger. Although he has a
strong, assertive personality, his faulty strategy has made him a
negative hero. Olsen's weakness demonstrates that Benny Andersen
does not present a mere black and white picture of the interpersonal tensions created by social norms. Rather, he warns against
shirking the responsibility to reach out; at the same time, he

points out the difficulty of recognizing one's own position and
one's self-persuasion behind rational argumentation.

"Fats Olsen" illustrates how skillfully Andersen employs the
associative technique in presenting a "slice of life" structured
around a first person narrator as protagonist who permits us to
see an inside view and thereby also includes us in his isolation.
He subtly directs our point of view by means of a stream-of-
consciousness technique and can suddenly break out for an instant
and address us, as in "Fats Olsen," to appeal to our understanding
of the course of action he has chosen. We become witnesses of a
tense situation which continues beyond a climax and, in some
stories, is emphasized by a final ironic twist. "Fats Olsen,"
where collective and personal traumas are merged, has been
characterized--along with the other stories in this second
collection--as a case history from the hospital called Denmark in
the 1960's.[3] But to fault Andersen for not providing "suggestions
for treatment" along with his diagnosis,[4] is hardly justified, for
one of the major themes in Andersen's stories, besides the
development of the authentic person, is the necessity of genuine
communication on a varied everday scale.

8

Mirror Images: The Longer Narratives

In the longer narrative Svante's Songs (1972) and in the novel On the Bridge (1981), the dialectical pattern we have observed in Andersen's poetry and short prose is given a different kind of emphasis. The direction for this emphasis is already hinted at in "A Happy Person," the last story in Fats Olsen and Other Stories, in which the hero's double life demonstrates the challenge of a divided personality by means of an allegorical split.[1] Such a division is carried out fully in Andersen's longer narrative works and parallels the narrative approach he takes in his novels for children.

I Andersen's Point of View as an Author: Svante's Songs

At first glance, the title of Svante's Songs recalls the collections Fredman's Songs (Fredmans sånger) and Fredman's Epistles (Fredmans epistlar) of the eighteenth century Swedish poet and composer Carl Michael Bellman. In addition, literary critics have also pointed to affinities with Fun in Denmark (Sjov i Danmark, 1928) by the Danish writer Jens August Schade because of the social satire in Schade's and Andersen's works.[2] A closer look at Svante's Songs, however, reveals that the tale occuppies a special place in Andersen's literary production as one element in a coherent system.

In writing this documentary story, Andersen not only plays the role of editor; he also includes his own fictional persona--whom he calls Benny Andersen--as a counterpart to the protagonist Svante Svendsen. The two characters, who last saw each other at the time of their high school graduation, meet again around 1960, when Svante, a medical school dropout, is making his living by writing a medical advice column for a newspaper. With his negative reactions to the established patterns of life around him, to the rushed pace of modern Danish society oriented toward an abundance of commodities and advertisements, Svante lives up to the traditional image of the Romantic poet who is suffering from society and withdrawing to his rented room to write poetry. His poems are composed in the simple style of the folksong and express the difficulties he has with department stores and with keeping his lover Nina to himself. They reveal his nostalgia for a harmonious pastoral life untouched by the demands of society, but instead revolving around love and simple commodities such as a beer or morning coffee. For Svante, this ideal becomes synonymous with his native Sweden although he has not been back since he left it at the age of nine. He disappears suddenly in 1971, after his old acquaintance Benny Andersen--a Modernist poet and a musician--has set those melancholic poems to music and, over their controversy about the poet's role in society, has announced that he will find a publisher for Svante's songs.

In his documentary retrospective on the ten years before Svante's disappearance, the fictitious Andersen juxtaposes their entirely different opinions about the role of the author in society. He reproaches Svante for his alleged withdrawal from social problems, enumerating a series of complex issues like pollution, overpopulation, napalm in Vietnam, drug problems, racial discrimination, slums, the Common Market, and the women's movement among others, to finally confront him with the question: "We live in 1971, and you are still writing about your small private petit-bourgeois provincial you, about unhappy love--can't you see those problems are a luxury?"[3]

Given the nature of Andersen's previous works, it is obvious that he is playing a role here. By acting as a mouthpiece for those critics who slight the importance of seemingly small private difficulties, Andersen is contrasting Svante's apparently anachronistic attitude toward life and poetry with demands for an author's social engagement. With Svante's outsider figure, he presents, on the one hand, a revaluation of traditionally rhymed poetic forms underscoring their complexity and their right to coexist along with the poetic experiments of Modernism; on the other hand, through Svante's tragicomic efforts to cope with life, Andersen voices an open protest against the rapid pace of a well-functioning society in which individuality, including the author's, is forced into conforming to a rigid system of normative values. Through his poems, opinions and behavior, Svante appears as an anachronism to the modern society he lives in, much too slow in his pace of living and deciding and completely thrown off balance by the flood of consumer goods and advertisements in department stores. He has become an outsider because he cannot integrate himself, because he is looking for the genuine in life

on an everyday scale, in the simple things and in every aspect of
communication. His feeling of not wanting to keep up with the
pace around him, his suspicion that Nina exchanges him with other
men, consumes him, only leads to further self-isolation and
depression.

While Svante's weariness of his environment constitutes a
criticism of Danish society, it must also be seen as a transitional stage in his life as symbolized by his position between
extremes: rejecting   participation   in Danish society while
idealizing Sweden from a distance. After all, he does not dare
face this Sweden and avoids going there under the pretext of
getting seasick or, more likely, because he expects to suffer from
existential nausea on the ferry between Copenhagen and Malmö.
Even though he is an emigrant from modern urban society, his
protesting withdrawal into an inner exile, at times with an
overdose of self-pity, amounts to escapism.   We can sympathize
with Svante when he insists on being himself--on being only a
shadow of himself rather than "a shadow of others." (61) But
Svante also neglects to create a balance between his subjective
reality and that around him. That it is possible for him to interact with others and still be himself can be seen from his conversation with a street vendor of hot-dogs to whom Svante
describes in lengthy detail the hot-dog he would have ordered if
he still liked hot-dogs. From a conventional point of view,
Svante's deviant behavior might even be termed absurd because it
merely wastes the time of the man who tries to sell hot-dogs. The
vendor, however, adjusts to Svante's perspective, and every
evening until Svante again likes hot-dogs he helps the poet choose
what he might have bought. These scenes demonstrate that Svante
could be himself, since tolerance can override the purely functional provided that he gives up his isolation. An adjustment is
necessary on the part of both the individual and society if normative values are to serve a humane social climate rather than the
mere upholding of efficiency. If this basic challenge is ignored,
how can a humane solution to large-scale problems be found? This
is clearly a major question raised by Svante's story. Seen in the
light of the difficulties Svante has been preoccupied with, we can
recognize the tongue-in-cheek quality of his response to being
faulted by Benny Andersen for an anachronistic attitude toward an
author's function in society. When challenged to admit that he
would like to have his songs published, Svante counters: "Why
should I exhibit my private petit-bourgeois effusions? Who should
be interested in problems that are my private luxury?" (66)

By playing the role of Svante's critic, Andersen defends the
author's right to self-determination concerning the choice of issues and a critical perspective. He points out the importance of
small everyday problems, which he considers by no means as
detached from those on a larger scale, as the calls for a socially
engaged literature would have us believe. Andersen seems to react
here to those critics who demanded the treatment of contemporary
social and political issues in literature yet criticized writers
for not providing solutions.[4]

As can be seen from the enormous success of Svante's Songs in
Denmark, the book and the music struck a highly responsive cord in

the public which apparently identified with Svante's difficulties. His objections to the quality of life and to the attitudes of literary critics should not, however, distract us from his escapism. He must develop away from the phase of self-contained opposition he is in. When he disappears before his reclusive life is made public through his songs, there is an indication that he will make a development toward balancing his dominant in- dividualistic views with the reality around him. Not only does the fictitious Andersen speculate that Svante decided to return and face Sweden; the poem Svante left behind also suggests such a turn, despite its ambiguity: "Behind me are misused days./ Before me something I don't know." (69) Svante departs without bitterness and with wishes of songs and love for those he leaves behind. He must face his challenge alone, and the realization of "misused days" in his past points to at least his attempt to end a phase of his development.

Among Andersen's characters, Svante is the one who, beyond a number of external traits, bears the closest resemblance to Sartre's hero Roquentin. Neither one of them is considered hand- some, each experiences having the woman in his life leave him for other men, and each leads a solitary existence in a rented room-- hiding behind his writing while feeling an overwhelming aversion to bourgeois life around him. In addition, each attempts to come to terms with his past and present life, finally realizing that, while misused days lie behind him, a challenge waits ahead of him; this realization prompts each of them to leave the city in which he was so miserable. Svante could easily join Roquentin in stating: "I too have wanted to be," have been motivated by the desire to "drive existence out of me;"[5] and he could, as well, join in with Roquentin's conclusion that his experiences "could even serve as a fable" about "a poor fellow who had got into the wrong world."

> He existed, like other people, in the world of municipal parks, of bistros, of ports, and he wanted to convince himself that he was living somewhere else, behind the canvas of paintings, with the doges of Tintoretto, with Gozzoli's wor- thy Florentines, behind the pages of books, with Fabrice del Dongo and Julien Sorel, behind gramophone records, with the long dry laments of jazz music. And then, after making a complete fool of himself, he understood, he opened his eyes, he saw that there had been a mistake: he was in a bistro, in fact, in front of a glass of warm beer. He sat there on the bench, utterly depressed; he thought: I am a fool. And at that very moment, on the other side of existence, in that other world which you can see from a distance, but without ever approaching it, a little melody started dancing, started singing: 'You must be like me; you must suffer in strict time.'[6]

The analogy is striking. Svante, too, "had got into the wrong
world," exists, like other people, in a world of city streets,
department stores, hot-dog carts, and solitary rented rooms, with
a bottle of warm porter in front of him, while living in a dream-
world of pastoral landscapes. His poem "Longing for Sweden"
("Længsel efter Sverige"), in particular, reflects his attempt to
settle into a world of phantasy, into a place and time of a bygone
Golden Age, "the promised land/.../where time hardly has lost its
bite / and where people sing Bellman-songs / with lingonberries in
their mouths / in light birch groves." (30) Although Svante has
kept well informed about modern Swedish society, he has been
unable to reconcile the childhood image of his native country with
the reality of contemporary Sweden. He can be suspected of
wanting to settle into his refuge of poetic Weltschmerz by having
his poems set to music, thus hiding behind the "laments" of the
songs composed by his friend Benny, whose music matches the
shifting moods, and the degree of suffering in Svante's lyrics,
especially in the case of the dragging jazz rhythm in "Svante"s
dark song" ("Svantes sorte vise"). But his friend functions like
the challenging voice Roquentin hears, because Benny, the poet and
musician, who lives with his own emotional upheavals caused by
family matters and sociopolitical problems, confronts Svante with
the imperative to "suffer in strict time," here and now, by facing
modern society. Svante must choose to give up his one-sided interest in his pleasure and comfort; he must choose to suffer on a
broader scale than the merely subjective, solipsistic one.
Besides, Benny Andersen convinces Svante with his action, not so
much with his arguments, because he takes away Svante's refuge by
having the songs published. Svante's songs thereby become independent of Svante and begin their own suffering "in strict
time," leaving Svante to take the leap himself and depart for the
unknown in a concrete as well as in a figurative sense. Svante
had hinted at this challenge himself when he wrote in his "Dark
Song" ("Sorte vise"): "It would be nice if you could forget / who
you are and be born again." (52) For this reason, it is fair to
assume that Svante has decided to face this challenge of "coming
into the world" by his own choice and to stop existing "with the
help of others" (10) as he did in the past.
    In Svante's Songs, Andersen's dialectical stance as author is
visible, for he demonstrates the link between the individual and
the social dimension and how they each need to transcend the extreme and complement each other. By contrasting Svante--who
represents his ever-present individualistic side--with the well-
known public side of his personality, Andersen alludes to the
balancing act he himself is engaged in.

            II Between Times: On the Bridge

    Compared to Andersen's short stories, his novel On the Bridge
--like his novels for children--mirror the transition to a more
tranquil narrative stance. Here we do not encounter a negative

hero who directs our focus to one preoccupying thought which he enlarges in proportion to his desperation; nor do we find a detached narrator's analysis of the tension surrounding a protagonist, as in some of the later stories. Instead, we are captured by the immediacy of the fourteen-year-old Erling's expectations of life, as juxtaposed with his emotionally detached perspective as an adult several decades later.

By placing into the novel's center the fundamental process of individual development, Andersen builds on the main themes of his earlier work, in which the hero is frequently torn between being himself and wanting to be somebody in accordance with established social norms. Although the novel's scope is limited by its time span, it bears close resemblance to the genre of the Bildungsroman. In an expansion on the contrasting technique of Svante's Songs, Andersen represents the opposite possibilities of integration according to social directives on the one hand, and self-realization as a first step for meaningful social integration on the other, by personifying these attitudes in the friends Erling and Allan respectively. During their one-and-a-half year long friendship, we encounter the dialectical pattern of individual conflict so characteristic of Andersen's literary production. While the figure of Allan has biographical traits of Andersen himself--apart from having been given Andersen's middle name, Allan's social milieu coincides with Andersen's working class home in Søborg--Erling represents Andersen's ethical point of view as it has been present ever since the first volume of poetry, The Musical Eel. We can therefore consider the adult Erling's retrospective account as Andersen's look at his own duality as he experienced and perceived it with growing consciousness.

With the figure of Erling, we are introduced to a budding personality in the middle of puberty and are shown the mixture of wonder, curiosity, and suspense he experiences at the traditional stage from child to young adult. As the first person narrator, Erling reveals to us a developing young mind open to life's complexities. At the same time, he presents his alter ego in his close friend Allan. While Erling admires Allan's strength and determination, he nevertheless feels the need to withdraw from Allan's influence. At first glance, the more single-minded Allan appears to dominate the more pliant Erling, but their friendship gradually becomes primarily a learning process for Erling. While he admires Allan and submits to his leadership, he also develops away from Allan's dominance and one-dimensional outlook on life the more he gets to know both Allan and himself.

Within a limited time span and the limited geographical area of Copenhagen's northwestern suburbs, a detailed traffic pattern between and around Allan's and Erling's houses--not only literally but also in an emotional sense--is drawn up before our eyes. In a series of episodes that take place from March to July of 1944, the novel depicts the last months of their friendship, a decisive transitional phase for Erling which, from his later perspective as narrator, was a period "on the bridge between the school years and an uncertain future."[7] It was a period of maturing, of growing insight into human nature and social processes, when graduation from school necessitated decisions about which direction to take for the future.   Historically, Denmark was isolated under the German occupation and experienced the beginning of the occupation's final phase.   Consequently, it was a time that resembled an incubation period, both from a personal and from an historical perspective. All the decisive developments are fused in the focus on Erling's personality as he gradually asserts himself with an emerging set of personal values.

Although coming to terms with oneself and others constitutes a fundamental challenge that has to be faced constantly, its complexity varies with each different socio-historical context.   In On the Bridge as well as elsewhere in his work, Andersen moves in closely on the dialectical process within the individual, and additionally on the role played by a primarily lower middle class environment. In the two ultimately conflicting forms of self-assertion represented by Erling and Allan, Allan's functional view is directed toward realizing his goals the tough, even aggressive way while Erling's more complex view is directed toward reconciling oppositions through an understanding of both sides as a basis for responsible action. Accordingly, Allan's hard line, his speed and self-confidence and his calculated technique in fist fights, lend him an image of strength in the daily power struggles. Since Erling, on the other hand, has a far greater sense of the complexity of his surroundings, most decisions are not as clear-cut for him, and he appears as the slower--at least as long as he submits to Allan's directives. The fact that he admires Allan's direct and successful approach, while also disagreeing with his inflexible attitude, indicates an inner conflict which mandates a solution of far-reaching implications.   He must take a stand in a social environment where an image of toughness and physical strength commands respect whereas even slight deviations from the norms of appearance or behavior expose a person to ridicule "in Hans Christian Andersen's country." The social climate depicted is reminiscent of Aksel Sandemose's critical view of petit-bourgeois Danish attitudes which he called "the law of Jante," named after the small town in his novel A Fugitive Crosses His Tracks   (En flyktning krysser sitt spor, 1933). Teachers and other children in Andersen's novel give vivid examples of senseless teasing, be it Ole's protruding eyes that are ridiculed or the appearance of Karen, the mulatto girl. Erling himself has a sensitive spot which leads him to identify with Karen's outsider position. His father was a sailor who drowned at sea in the Far East before he could marry Erling's mother.   Without a picture, only a self-made image of his father, Erling's search for a personal identity is intimately connected with his concern about fair and responsible treatment of others and by others. He needs to decide whether he wants to subscribe to the unwritten laws of social Darwinism already practiced in the children's interactions, and whether he wants to follow Allan's direction, integrate himself, and thus reproduce the very same tough stance that is valued highly by his environment.   His relationship with Allan resembles the struggles between the cowboys and Indians in Erling's comic books, and the symbolic picture he draws of the confrontation between the well-armed cowboy facing the disadvantaged Indian leaves the result of the battle unknown.

What we do know is that Erling is not the person to enjoy such battles but that he likes to explore the validity of the norms he is confronted with daily.

In his small daily world, Erling's growing independence is complemented by his increasing awareness of life's complexities, as we are shown in the streetcar episode of the novel's second chapter "Eyes, Glances." This chapter is paradigmatic both for the novel's theme and for its mode of narration, because the leitmotif of eyes and glances points to the visual plane on which the narrative moves in accordance with Erling's perception and growing consciousness. Here, a banal event on an overcrowded streetcar where Erling has to decide to whom, if at all, he should offer his seat, suddenly takes on special importance when it exemplifies how a humane ethical stance must be applied here and now, in what commonly is considered the unheroic everyday life. Confronted with the aggression of an ill-mannered little girl who is envious of his seat, Erling's wish to offer it to her tired-looking mother becomes a problem for him. He tries to balance his understanding with his irritation and his self-respect, only to be surprised by the unexpected reaction of another passenger. When the streetcar stops abruptly and the little girl with her angry eyes falls on an emaciated young man seated on the other side, even bending the pages in his book, Erling is struck by the overwhelming warmth and kindness in the man's eyes. The understanding and concern they reflect, above all the joy and love they transmit, contrast sharply with the man's sorry physical appearance. The glance from these eyes demonstrates to Erling on a small everyday scale how understanding and kindness are the key to softening confrontations. Erling feels to what extent it is possible to reach out with glances and provide joy.

Erling's receptivity to the moral significance of such experiences is at least in part the work of his mother. She has encouraged a sense of partnership between Erling and herself, giving him turns to take care of their small tobacco and newspaper shop. The small portions of self-confidence and self-esteem she provides him with along with her love and trust contribute to a sound ethical basis for Erling's personality. In the long run, it proves to be the genuinely powerful attitude, and by comparison, Allan's hard line cannot compete and actually proves to be rather brittle. Besides being tough, Allan longs for heroic self-realization on a large scale. This lends him the image of a daredevil but also leaves him highly dissatisfied, for he expects to find an occasion to prove himself wherever decisive historical events take place, but not here and now in his own environment. The myth of heroic action--at war or among cowboys and Indians--prevents him from seeing the chance for a less glamorous realization, the more immediate chance of being there for others that is exemplified by both Allan's and Erling's mothers. As if to underscore Allan's misdirected expectations, the exciting historical events come all the way to his front door when street fights break out between Danes and the German occupation forces, but while Allan is not at home.

With each episode in Erling's learning process, he develops more rapidly away from Allan and becomes more himself. Their conflicting views are especially evident when Erling goes along with Allan's decision to confront their parents with a speaking strike because he feels oppressed by them, and not to speak to anyone for twenty-four hours. In spite of his solidarity, Erling has scruples about treating his friends and his mother in such a way, precisely because he does not experience life as clearly divided into those who order and those who have to follow. When he is further supported in his doubts by the undeserved love and concern he receives as a result of not speaking--he is believed to be either mute or ill--he breaks out of this senseless solidarity. His motivation, here as well as in later episodes, is determined by his concern for others and the awareness that he acted wrongly. Unlike him, Allan is motivated in breaking off the strike, and will be in events later on, by a narrow focus on his own interests.

The title chapter "On the Bridge" functions as a turning point for the novel's thematic development and encompasses its major structural characteristics, the primarily visual mode of narration. On the first days of vacation after graduating from school, Allan, Erling and Birthe F. always meet at three o'clock in the afternoon on the bridge over the commuter train tracks at the suburban station of Vangede. It is always Allan and Birthe who are involved in a semi-hostile conversation about Birthe's girlfriend Lise, on whom Allan has a secret crush. Erling's presence merely serves to prevent any rumors about Allan and Birthe. The image of the bridge thus takes on a level of symbolic significance beyond that of interlude between school and an uncertain future. It also points to how Erling is being used as a communication bridge between Allan and Birthe without any appreciation for his person, just as he is used by Birthe's cat, simply as a stepping stone for crossing over to Allan. The repetitive traffic pattern of their meetings on the bridge comes to a halt for one moment when it dawns on Erling that the absent Lise actually is the center of attention. This moment of insight is frozen through a flashback whereby Allan's brief disappearance on a class trip the summer before is intercut into the present constellation on the bridge. With this visual juxtaposition, objective time is arrested momentarily to focus on Erling's subjective experience of time in accordance with his belated, very sudden understanding of the present situation and of Allan's emotional state. He further realizes that he has been used and that he has never been taken into Allan's confidence. He therefore no longer tries to keep up an appearance of being on the same wave-length as Allan but instead--weak or strong--simply is himself. When their communication deteriorates abruptly because of Allan's withdrawal after Birthe has announced Lise's rejection and ridicule of Allan's enamoredness, he begins to grasp how meaningless his relationship with Allan has become. As a personality, Allan remains isolated within himelf and his egocentric perspective, unable to take the risk of genuinely reaching out to others. At first Erling's protest against being used in such a manner remains on a private level. Not until after their expedition to stock up on bread when the Danish strike against the German occupation forces threatens food supplies in Copenhagen, do all doubts disappear in the realization that their differing attitudes cannot be bridged. During this expedition, Erling had been tossed off his bicycle and experienced a cathartic crying spell which, in its dimensions, did not match his fall but rather his pent-up inner tension. Following this symbolic toss off his bike, Erling's increased awareness of Allan's personality inevitably leads to their separation.

Allan's tough stance and self-imposed isolation grant him only the appearance of autonomy. As a form of short-sighted self-protection, such a one-dimensional approach to life has not prepared him to cope with conflicts he cannot fight out. In contrast to Erling, he therefore experiences only the negative aspects of their futile bicycle trip to the various bakeries in the area and sees neither the beauty of nature nor the sorry state of the German soldiers manning the check points--faces of tired elderly men or tense young faces their own age. Erling's comparison of Allan's tenseness with that of the young soldier who does not allow them to pass illustrates fear turned into aggression on both sides, an attitude which only promotes a harsh confrontation but is useless for resolving it. Erling's perception of the basic human attitude underlying the aggressive reaction of both boys, confirms for him a view which requires the acceptance of complexity.

Throughout the novel, but thematically emphasized at the end, this view is expressed by a contrastive pattern as visible in Erling's statement "unfortunately and luckily;" happy-sad, bittersweet, the brittleness of strength--these are some of the contrasts Erling finds coexisting and defying any simplistically unambiguous perspective, no matter how functional and widely accepted it may be. Relative strength and autonomy have to be sought by an open-minded acceptance of these complexities if a responsible and tolerant attitude is to be achieved. Erling is therefore not as easily thrown off balance when his expectations are disappointed, unless his code of ethics is affected; he does not approach life with rigid expectations. While Allan mirrors a side of human personality which is potentially there in Erling, as expressed in Erling's initial admiration, it is Erling who represents another potential that Allan has not developed.

Having managed to bypass the German checkpoint by sneaking through the Utterslev marsh in Copenhagen, both Erling and Allan sense the necessity of going their separate ways. Symbolically, Erling's process of growth is depicted by the few inches he has grown taller, by which, at least temporarily, he has outgrown Allan in height. The uncertain future has begun, historically with the General Strike of the Danes against the German occupation at the beginning of July 1944, and for Erling specifically because his struggle for an acceptable set of values passes into another phase by his withdrawal from Allan. At home, his self-assertion is documented further in the relationship with his mother in which the roles of child and adult now appear reversed: he is the one giving her support, easing her anxiety about his prolonged bread expedition on the other side of the German barricades; and he is the one who decides on the future course for his life--to continue his education in night school while working during the day. With this decision, Erling takes on recognizable autobiographical similarities to the author,[8] whereby his development suggests the ethical affinity between his attitude at the novel's end and Andersen's own view.

As much as the growth of Erling's personality is stressed in the novel, no doubt is left about the open nature of this process. Not until the third chapter does the narrator identify himself, when he signs his drawing with "Erling L." While Allan had used his first name in chapter one, he did so without addressing him by merely talking about him in his presence as if he were not there or as if his presence did not count. In the sixth chapter, when Erling has asserted himself by breaking the strike of not speaking and confronts Allan with his decision, Allan's mother addresses him with his first name. Finally, in the ninth and last chapter, this gradation culminates with Erling's strong, decisive attitude and self-acceptance:

> 'Erling,' I murmured to myself in the mirror. The name mother had called when she dreamt she was dying. In her greatest anguish, it was me she had called for, me and no one else!
> I felt so proud and tipsy with joy (...) that I had to make a few grotesque faces, make a little fun of myself, to be able to stand it.
> 'Erling Larsen,' I announced with a low deep voice. Corrected it to: 'Mr. Erling Larsen!'[9]

While the fourteen-year-old Erling has reached the point of starting a well-deserved new life at the end of the novel, we know nothing about the personal circumstances of the adult Erling whose narrative perspective has guided us. But since throughout his story, he has addressed us, his present contemporaries several decades later, we clearly know about his basic concern: to transmit the fundamental importance of developing a self-sufficient ethical stance independent of predominant narrow-minded attitudes. He demonstrates personal growth and self-acceptance as an essential beginning in this process, a coming to terms with oneself before being able to reach out to others. We recognize Andersen's ethical stance, the dialectical pattern of "coming into the world" and reaching out, not least through the warmth and kindness of glances, as a counter-position to self-centered escapism. It is the emphasis on individual development despite any still existing norms resembling the petit-bourgeois "law of Jante" in Sandemose's novel; and thus it constitutes a continuing challenge to the individual, linking the personal with the social for the sake of a humane social environment that must begin in the unheroic everyday realm. Around this basic concern, Andersen develops before us the maturing boy's world of sensitivities with carefully balanced psychological insight that has its equivalent in Danish literature in H. C. Branner's best short stories.[10]

III Mirror for an Adult World: The Children, Snøvs and
               the Cat in the Bag[11]

    At the center of Andersen's novels for children lies a divi-
sion into two worlds, and thereby into two different views of the
world, one of children and one of adults; they are not in rigid
opposition to each other but rather in need of complementing each
other, and it is the children who play the most active roles in
the search for that vanished dimension that separates the two
worlds.
    Through the children's experiences in Excuse me, Sir--where
is Nature?, Andersen mirrors a world of inverted values--that is,
he mirrors distortions of what is considered natural, normal, and
progressive insofar as the fabricated, the artificial, accompanied
by a lack of tolerance for the inefficient, have come to dominate
life.   Although such a view of daily life is familiar from Svante's Songs it is no longer presented as the subjective view of an
isolated individual; instead, it characterizes a general state of
the world that has taken on a futuristic appearance.
    "Excuse me, sir, but do you know where the nature is?"[12] two
eight-year-old Danish children ask in their best schoolbook
English, only to encounter a negative answer from an Australian.
The year is 2000, when all of Denmark has become one big city;
there are regular connections to remote but equally monotonous
parts of the globe which only take the time span of at the most
four movies in a windowless rocket train, and vacation specials
readily make available a trip to the moon in all its phases or an
affordable shopping spree to Saturn, where space outfits are especially cheap at the time.
    There are perhaps more thrilling, breathtaking or horrifying
visions of the upcoming turn of the century than the one outlined
in Excuse me, Sir-where is Nature?, but the vision that nature is
an almost extinct locality, barely known through hearsay, is
thought-provoking for at least two reasons: The first is that it
is largely based on ideas contributed by children to a cooperative
venture called "børnelytterroman," (children's radio novel) undertaken by Benny Andersen and Danmarks Radio in 1973, at a time when
audience or reader involvement had become a part of literary practice and discussion. The second reason is that Andersen's role in
guiding the contributions sent to the radio by the children, who
listened to the sequels, is indicative of his own commitment as a
writer; this role links the radio novel with his other stories for
children, the three volumes which focus on a most phantastic creature called snøvs, and it links these books with his works in
other genres as well.
    Within his oeuvre, Andersen's novels for children can be said
to occupy a very special place, because they contain, in a nut-
shell, all his essential themes. Here, we find his commitment to
the natural, simple things of childhood integrated into his
ethical imperative of "coming into the world," of reaching out to
others in an effort of creating a more humane world, a
"moreworld," beginning with our immediate surroundings. Here, we
can also best observe how Andersen's experimentation with

language, his creation of "unsprayed idioms," serves to express the thematic complexity he has developed, which involves--beyond individual existential balance--sociopolitical and, more specifically, ecological balance.

In the radio novel, Excuse me, Sir- where is Nature? , the rather chilling vision of the future sketches a society whose belief in progress and technology has led to the creation of an environment that can be characterized as one of pervasive cold-ness. Andersen combines his skeptical and protesting attitude toward such progress with actual observations made by Danish children in 1973 --observations delineating an undesirable trend toward a world that displays affluency in technology but poverty in nonmaterialistic values such as human warmth, joy, and love. A one-dimensional life has evolved based on artificiality and sig-nifying a serious loss of existential balance; not only is nature being deprived of its existence, but people are being deprived of nearly everything natural in their environment: The planet Earth is coated with concrete, topped with more concrete and steel, and in some places, its sky is decorated with plastic birds. Food consists of differently colored pills, which, only after having dissolved in stomach fluids, indicate by way of a slight burp the taste and possible substance they contained. The minor officials representing this society, such as policemen and bus and train conductors, tend to be efficient and versatile robots.

In contrast to this critical stage of development, one last mysterious patch of land called nature has survived somewhere far off around Aarhus on the East coast of Jutland. It becomes the focus of the novel, when Andersen and his young listeners have their heroes, two eight-year-old Danish children named Jo and Ivan, attempt to break out of an unbalanced existence and try to find nature, or more precisely, to find the walled-in farm, fields, and meadows where Jo's uncle is still holding out. Through this stark contrast of fabricated versus natural environ-ment, the novel not only diagnoses the system as damaging to human nature but also protests the current trends we as citizens allow our societies to pursue in the direction of what can be termed a "false nature," to borrow Roland Barthes' formulation.[13]

Based on the myth of progress that equates advances in science and technology with a guaranteed improvement of the human condition, adults have created and are supporting an environment of which they also have become victims. As in the case of Jo's mother and Ivan's father, they are seen as unhappy individuals in a cold, efficiency-oriented world, isolated even from their chil-dren, without joy and warmth. The radio novel--after portraying such a reduced existence--reverses the development by literally importing those submerged values. Warmth is symbolized by Italian sun, at first still in cans from Italy; but when Jo, her uncle, and her friend Ivan are joined by the entire family of a former Italian guest worker, Italian warmth, togetherness, and joy of life spread to encompass family as well as friends and, together, they initiate a nature-movement. As it grows, the movement offers a balance to "progress" by expanding nature and spreading the joy in simple things of life; it also promotes in people an awareness of their surroundings which helps the parents of Jo and Ivan to transcend their isolation. Andersen's didactic gesture points in the direction of the thematic complex mentioned earlier: individual as well as social balance--the latter is to be understood as balanced interpersonal relationships--rest on a balance of values and norms, regardless of national boundaries. It further-more demonstrates a kind of European cooperation quite contrary to that of the EEC, which Andersen opposes in some of his other works.[14] In addition, Jo's role as the initiator of the search for nature emphasizes the importance of active individual commitment to existential balance.

This basic theme is clothed in a series of adventurous ex-periences of the children in Andersen's books and usually focuses on the individual's level, as in the case of Andersen's snøvsen-trilogy. Although Andersen's young heroes always start out because they sense that something is wrong, is lacking, is out of balance, their sincere motivation is often communicated in a very humorous way because, as children, they enjoy, and suffer from, a less complete perspective of their surroundings. This may be con-sidered a disadvantage, because it may be bewildering and scary, or it may be considered an advantage, because it defies the routine perception and thus perhaps discouragement. In any case, it provides a fresh look at human relationships and values. In this respect, Andersen's trilogy around snøvs constitutes a veritable guide to meaningful social interaction, because seeing an other person--not merely in a particular social role, but also as a more complex person wanting to live a full life--is practised by snøvs and the children. Andersen cleverly manages to include both adults and children in his model world by inventing the phan-tastic figure of snøvs whose name is derived from the idiom "at gå fra snøvsen" (I, 15), literally: 'to go away from the snøvs,' meaning 'to go crazy.' His strategy of presenting snøvs as an in-dividualistic little creature is based on the fact that snøvs by himself makes no sense, neither as a word nor as the little crea-ture bearing such a name.

When the seven-year-old Eigil in book one of the snøvsen-trilogy hears that "everybody has gone crazy" after they first "have bought the cat in the bag" (English: the pig in the poke), he sets out to find snøvs and the cat. His primary motiva-tion is compassion for that poor mysterious person called snøvs, from whom everyone has gone away and whose isolation, fear, and existential loneliness Eigil can well imagine. Andersen cor-relates it with Eigil's experience on an evening some years ear-lier when he woke up after his parents had gone out and felt totally isolated in the dark, in a veritable existential crisis. Through this correlation, snøvs comes to symbolize the isolated individual and personifies existential loneliness--after all, he is unique in the world--, but because of the idiom from which he is created, his isolation is not depicted as negative. It is not the self-inflicted isolation we so often find in Andersen's poems and stories; rather, the problem lies with the behavior of the rest of the world, because everybody has gone away from him, and everybody has thereby lost his head, gone crazy. And the first to always go away from snøvs are, in his own testimony, the police, since "they have so much to look after." (I, 18) The irony in this excuse can hardly be overlooked, although it is by no means just a witty, side-tracking stab at certain authorities who enforce the laws of society. Like most adults, these authorities represent attitudes and behavior patterns founded on a restricted perspective of, for instance, either right or wrong, either good or bad, etc. Snøvs, on the other hand, serves as a reminder of the complexity of existence, pointing out constantly the crude and reductive oversimplification of what is perhaps an efficient, but also a narrow approach to life. Whose fault is it, for example, that Eigil cannot find his way home after having searched for and found snøvs, this modern Tom Thumb who ventures through life on one big toe? It is everybody's fault, since "everybody had gone crazy." (I, 51) Furthermore, it is everyone's fault that Eigil set out to find first snøvs and then the cat; as the story shows, however, it is very good that the three of them met, for snøvs teaches Eigil-- and also Andersen's readers--how to regard an issue in many different ways and how to perceive that which is genuinely important. Through snøvs, then, Andersen emphasizes the significance of sharing a variety of viewpoints in order to arrive at some insight into what is really important in life.

While the experiences of Eigil, snøvs, and the cat provide a close-up view of the often startling behavior of adults, the need for an objective distance is suggested to the reader through the comments of the cat, who states, "Humans are interesting beings, indeed. If I get rich some time, I'll acquire some humans to study their strange behavior" (I, 76). A key example of this strange human behavior is witnessed by snøvs when he accompanies Eigil and their friend Pernille to the movies to watch a Laurel and Hardy (Gøg og Gokke) film. Here, Andersen demonstrates in his books for children what he meant by the challenge voiced in one of his earliest poems in which the speaker states: "The ridiculous I want to take seriously."[15] That is exactly what snøvs does as he views Laurel (Gøg) being mistreated by Hardy (Gokke). Stan Laurel, of course, since he is ridiculed and thus allows spectators to feel superior, is consistently the cause of fits of laughter in the cinema. Snøvs, on the other hand, looks beyond the ridiculous, perceiving Laurel as the one who is isolated by everyone's laughter after first having been treated cruelly by Hardy. Snøvs' open protest against the fact that Hardy constantly hits Laurel, making him cry and still having the laughter on his side, amounts to a protest against cruelty accepted because it looks funny. He succeeds in creating an awareness of something faulty in people's behavior, that is, in their way of looking at others as well as at themselves, because he can convince Pernille and Eigil that they need to expand and thus balance their perspectives (III, 56-57). They should rather be laughing at themselves for having chosen to accept put-down humor and thereby having affirmed denigration at the expense of humane treatment of others.

Andersen's creation of snøvs could be termed analogous to the biblical creation according to John, for in the beginning was the Word, that is, the idiom, from which snøvs and his world evolved. While snøvs lives in a world of his own dreams, fears, errors, and good intentions, his unconventional perspective underscores the complexity of life; he transmits psychological insight into

present-day human behavior that Andersen depicts as being in need
of balancing. Snøvs, always in need of balance himself, brings to
mind the speaker of the poem "Toddler" ("Tumling"), whose attempts
to balance and grow he shares; in contrast to his mainly
theoretical presentation in "Toddler," Andersen places snøvs into
easily recognizable situations taken from everyday life. Andersen
thus presents an approach to daily interaction, which he usually
depicts in his other works as absent in contemporary society. The
dialectics of life, the process of becoming by means of suffering,
seeing, and trusting--as best exemplified in the parable-like poem
"Blanket-Toss"--, the choice of "being" over "existing," is also
indicated by Svante's disappearance, by Erling's breaking away
from Allan, and especially by the actions in Andersen's novels for
children.

In the latter, the imagination, and thereby a great deal of
what the adult world views as "impossible," has been given a full
range of development, on the linguistic level as well, where
imagination does not hesitate to reverse the meaning of standard
social conceptualizations, such as "to go crazy." These changes,
carried out by a free imagination, not only aim at two different
groups of recipients but also reveal a particular challenge.
Speaking to children, the stories create an awareness of desirable
values in life at a highly impressionable stage of childhood, when
there is still a great deal of confidence in the potential of each
person for creating an impact on the environment. Speaking at the
same time to adults, the stories present them with a mirror of
their own world including its desirable as well as its damaging
aspects. Both groups should be able to perceive the discernable
challenge: if the children are to be prevented from becoming a
part of that mirror image of an adult world, these two audiences
must joint in a united effort to enlarge that world. Andersen
thus demonstrates in his children's novels that his popular innovative word play goes well beyond a joy in linguistic games, for
by taking language at its word, he communicates his ethical concerns, addressing, like his famous countryman Hans Christian Andersen, both children and adults.

9

Conclusion

Benny Andersen is generally associated with the first post-war phase of Danish Modernism, in which the individual is characteristically portrayed in confrontation with the mechanics of society.[1] Probing more deeply into Andersen's poetry, the critic Finn Stein Larsen classifies it, along with that of Rifbjerg, Malinovski, Ørnsbo, and Sonne, as "poetry for everyday use" ("brugskunst") or "poetry of cognition" ("erkendelsespoesi").[2] While the qualities denoted by these misleading terms are by no means exclusive to the work of those five poets, the choice of terminology was meant to mark a departure in Danish poetry from the enclosed subjective Symbolism of the Heretica group. Essentially, Stein Larsen was identifying in the poetry of these five authors a technique for unmasking living conditions or human attitudes, a technique which can also be observed in Andersen's fiction and radio plays. In The Musical Eel, Andersen had written that he wanted to take the ridiculous seriously, and we might take this statement both as a motto for his work and as an indication of the unconventional perception that is the basis of his comic strategy in the various genres. Andersen has contributed significantly to exploring modern daily life by placing at the center of attention human types and typical situations, thus exposing the problem of the universal challenge of self-development within the inhibiting framework of a highly industrialized and prosperous society. Like his contemporary, the writer and philosopher Villy Sørensen, Andersen is preoccupied in his works with the confrontation between the individual and society, and with the common experience of angst and nothingness and with the many self-deluding strategies available to the individual who chooses not to attempt the development of his or her own personality. Both Villy Sørensen and Benny Andersen have learned from the way Hans Christian Andersen used language "to transform the banal everyday world into an inner poetic universe where even objects assume a significance while still remaining objects."[3] And although this is more readily apparent in Andersen's poetry, it is nevertheless subtly present in his prose as well, where objects can serve to mirror people's attitudes, fears, and evasions.

It has been maintained in this study that there is an underlying ethical system in Andersen's work, implicit at first, but gradually becoming more and more explicit in his most recent writing. However, because implicitness has been so characteristic of Andersen's diction, it would not be difficult for the reader of a particular poem or story to become absorbed in the tragicomic depiction or the, often ironic, word play, and thus miss the writer's call for individual responsibility which may explain why the reception of Andersen's works has focused pre-dominantly on their amusing aspects. But careful reading--and consideration of Andersen's entire literary production will enable the reader to comprehend that even those whimsical poems which illuminate a sad and amusing situation have at their base a unifying code of ethics.

In fact, Andersen has always had to work against the image of himself as a popular humorist and has frequently stressed his dislike of being restricted by such labels. Closer to the truth, he states, is the characterization that his writing is "amusing in a sad way or sad in an amusing way."[4] Still, the fact that he writes with a sense of humor may be the reason why Andersen struck a sympathetic chord with such a large number of readers and is more widely read than many modern Danish authors, even though these readers must eventually have realized that their laughter was directed against themselves. While it is understandable that Andersen might become annoyed at being labelled a humorist, he surely knows--as Kierkegaard did--that a writer who wants to change people's attitudes must meet them on their own grounds,[5] and this he has accomplished successfully through his tragicomic texts. His comic strategy, while creating a distance on the one hand, functions on the other as a barometer for the degree of seriousness of individual alienation. But Andersen is not content with diagnosing the collective traumas and the individual's contribution to them. In the face of a clearly acknowledged Kafkaesque situation, he goes beyond a self-ironizing attitude, especially in his later works, to transcend the confrontation. His focus on the mutual influencing of the individual and society contributes to the reader's awareness of how deeply entrenched we are in mechanical social processes. The sudden awakening to the dissatisfaction with a routine life is frequently indicated in Andersen's poetry and fiction by the sudden imbalance which occurs when the speaker or protagonist is tossed out of the daily routine. Andersen thus delineates the beginning of consciousness as described by Camus in The Myth of Sisyphus or as expressed in Sartre's existential nausea. The link between Andersen's works and Sartre's early novel Nausea is especially understandable, con-

sidering the fact that Kierkegaard's works were of significant influence for both writers. Andersen demonstrates as well how, like
Dostoevsky's underground man, we create our own hell, and that we
must recognize the extent to which misleading values govern our
daily life. With his close-ups of seemingly unheroic everyday existence, Andersen has placed his humanistic ideals of tolerance,
love, and mutual confidence in the sphere where they must first be
realized through development of the individual personality.   He
focuses not on the monumental courageous effort, but on the small
acts of courage required for conscious everyday life.

     In contrast to Naturalist or Existentialist writers who have
tended to alienate many of their readers because of their emphasis
on the ugly, gloomy, and tragic aspects of life, Andersen, with
his tragicomic approach, tricks the reader into a reception of his
philosophy through the appeal of the comic, the ironic, and the
satiric even at the risk that might allow the reader to escape into a one-dimensional mode of reception and merely seek entertain-
ment or even identification.[6] Andersen has, however, taken a major
step in reaching out to his audience with his first novel,
On the Bridge, published in the fall of 1981. His comic exaggeration has receded here in favor of a more direct mode of presenting
his ethical concerns. Although a tendency in this direction could
already be detected in the last two volumes of poetry, Under Both Eyes and Blanket-Toss, the novel explicitly develops an
applied Existentialist ethic by defining personal development and
genuine interaction with others against a background of our most
familiar everyday situations. Whether or not his audience is by
now willing to accept directly the ethical messages of Denmark's
"wisest and most radical author of conscience"[7]--and to meet him
on his own ground--remains to be seen.

     Throughout this study, the term "strategy" has been applied
to Andersen's literary and ethical approach to his audience, and
that term probably ought to replace the rather ponderous word
"system." Andersen, after all, does not construct any all-
encompassing solutions to life's problems, but rather offers suggestions for a more humane and personally fulfilling life. Like
the French Existentialists, he emphasizes the individual's responsibility for making the choices that will affect the direction of
his life; but instead of devising a Kierkegaardian system designed
to lead to salvation, he presents an ethical approach for the individual which may serve as a starting point toward a more authentic life.   In so doing, he fulfills his own responsibility as an
author committed to the furtherance of humanistic ideals in his
society, a responsibility which was the subject of heated debate
among postwar Danish intellectuals. At this point in his career,
it can be said that Benny Andersen's contribution to Danish
literature--and, indeed, to Western culture--lies in his ethical
commitment to the individual's realization of a balance between
personal needs and the demands of society and in the challenging
dialectical strategy through which he communicates this commitment.

Notes and References

* Albert Camus, "La Nausée by Jean-Paul Sartre," Lyrical and Critical, trans. Philip Thody (London, 1967), p. 147.

Chapter One

1. See Andersen's interview with Else Steen Hansen, "Mørklødede Cynthia har fornyet Benny Andersen," Aktuelt, April 26, 1978, for his comments regarding "To a Strong Man" from the collection Under begge øjne ; see also the analysis of "The Pillows" in ch. 6, sect. 5 of this book.

2. Benny Andersen, Selected Poems, trans. Alexander Taylor (Princeton, 1975), p. 87.

3. For a discussion of Abell's contribution to Danish drama, the reader is referred to Frederick J. Marker, Kjeld Abell, (TWAS 394) Boston: G. K. Hall, 1976.

4. Ole Wivel, "Kunst, Etik, Religion," Heretica 5 (1952), p. 149.

5. Dialog, 1950-61, followed Athenæum, which had appeared from 1946 until 1949.

6. Erik Knudsen, "Kunst, Moral, Politik," Heretica 5 (1952), p. 162.

7. "Humanisme og idedebat: Den intellektuelle mellem kultur og barbari," Dialog 3, 5/6 (1953), p. 4.

8. Finn Stein Larsen, "Lyrik," Modernismen i dansk litteratur ,
ed. J. Vosmar (Copenhagen, 1969), p. 17-18.

9. See Andersen's statement in the interview with Kjeld Rask
Therkilsen, "Det er med ord som med børn--de har godt af at tumle
sig," Berlingske Tidende, October 14, 1962.

10. "Thelonius Monk," Kamera med køkkenadgang, 3rd ed. (Copenhagen, 1965), pp. 68-69.

11. Nomader med noder (Copenhagen, 1976)

12. Ibid., p. 7.

13. See note 9, above; see also Thorkild Borup Jensen, "Benny Andersen," Danske Digtere i det 20. Århundrede, eds. F. Nielsen and
O. Restrup (Copenhagen, 1966), 3:677.

14. Ibid.; see also Barnet der blev ældre og ældre (Copenhagen,
1973), p. 18.

15. Niels Barfoed, "Benny Andersen: Den musikalske ål," Vindrosen 7 (1960), p. 586.

16. See, e.g., Torben Brostrøm, "Den nye bølge i lyrikken," Information, June 8, 1960.

17. These views are expressed in Digtere og dæmoner (Copenhagen,
1959), especially in the essays "Stat og personlighed," pp.
216-218, and "Velfærdsstat og personlighed," pp. 219-227.

18. "Sommerdag," Den musikalske ål (Copenhagen, 1960), p. 37.

19. "In the Bar," Selected Poems, p. 69

20. For a detailed account see "Der gik en ko på Vesterbro," Barnet der blev ældre og ældre, pp. 56-61. As a forerunner to Benny
Andersen, the Danish writer Halfdan Rasmussen can be named because
of his similar use of language in his numerous collections of Tos-
serier.

21. Nikke Nikke Nambo og andre danske børnerim og remser (Copenhagen, 1963); Lille Peter Dille og andre udenlandske børnerim
og remser (Copenhagen, 1964).

22. Hans Magnus Enzensberger, Allerleirauh. Viele schöne Kin-
derreime. (Frankfurt/M., 1961).

23. "Der gik en ko på Vesterbro," Barnet der blev ældre og ædre ,
p. 60.

24. Niels Barfoed has also noted a continuity here; see his
reviews "At indvinde ny svimmelhed," Information, September 23,
1969, and "Et, du er den!," Politiken, October 9, 1966.

25. In addition, Torben Brostrøm suggests that an affinity to the eighteenth century satirical novel, narrated from the point of view of a foreign explorer or scientist, is as much visible as that to the idyls of Goethe and Voss. "Reservatet Danmark," Information, August 24, 1971.

26. See, e.g., Erik Thygesen, "Andersens nationale særpræg," Politiken, August 24, 1971.

27. For a detailed discussion of Kolde fødder, see the edition in Rhodos Dramaserie (Copenhagen, 1980).

28. Prominent examples are the essays by Martin A. Hansen, "Eneren og massen," and by H. C. Branner, "Humanismens krise," in Mennesket i tiden (Copenhagen, 1950).

29. Andersen stressed Kierkegaard as one of his sources for inspiration in a discussion with American students in Copenhagen, June 25, 1980.

30. Tom Kristensen must be mentioned here with his review "Fra musikalsk til elektrisk ål," Politiken, November 24, 1962, and Niels Barfoed, with a later review, "At indvinde ny svimmelhed," Politiken, September 23, 1969.

Chapter Two

1. Selected Poems, p. 315. All page references in the text are to this bilingual edition, hereafter identified as SP; in all other cases, the translations are my own, and a reference to their Danish originals will be given.

2. Søren Kierkegaard's Journals and Papers, ed. and trans. Howard V. Hong and Edna H. Hong (Bloomington-London, 1970 and 1975), vol. 2, p. 529:No. 2276 and vol. 3, p. 257:No.2830.

3. Ole Wivel, "Jysk sonet," Digte 1948-58 (Copenhagen, 1960), p. 105. Page numbers in the text refer to this edition.

4. "Lige før vinter," Den musikalske ål, p. 30; the rhyme scheme of the Danish original could not be kept in the English translation.

5. Rainer Maria Rilke, "Herbst," Das Buch der Bilder (Leipzig, 1913), p. 52. The English version reads: "Yet there is One, with ever-gentle hand, / . . ., upholding all." T.C.C.: a College Miscellany, No. 926 (Tralee, 1946), p. 59.

6. "Novemberdag," Den musikalske ål, p. 38.

7. "Kryb," ibid., p. 28.

8. Ibid.

9. In his interview with Mette Ejlersen, Andersen also suggested that we should see the small wonders which happen around us every day; "De spiller på flere af livets strenge," Berlingske Tidende , August 13, 1961.

10. "Flaskeskipper," Den musikalske ål, p. 48.

11. See Niels Barfoed, "Benny Andersen: Den musikalske ål," Vindrosen 7 (1960), p. 586.

12. "Nye stemmer," Den musikalske ål, p. 43.

13. "Sult," Den musikalske ål, pp. 61-62. All page references in the text, following quotations from this poem and the other three prose poems, are to this edition.

14. Hugo von Hofmannsthal, "Das Gespräch über Gedichte," Ausgewählte Werke (Frankfurt/M., 1967), vol. 2, p. 378.

15. Ibid., p. 367.

16. Max Brod, Franz Kafka. Eine Biographie (New York, 1946), 2nd ed., p. 59: "Der Geruch nasser Steine in einem Hausflur" ("The smell of wet tiles in a hallway").

17. Roland Barthes, "Myth Today," _Mythologies_,   trans. Annette
Lavers (New York, 1978), pp. 109-159.

18. Jean-Paul Sartre, _Existentialism and Human Emotions_   (New
York, 1957), p. 29.

Chapter Three

1. _Existentialism and Human Emotions_, pp. 23-28.

2. These poems appeared in _Kamera med køkkenadgang_. All page references following my translations in the text are to the third edition (Copenhagen, 1965).

3. Poul Borum, "Skarp lud til de skurvede hoveder," _Jyllands-Posten_, Nov. 2, 1962.

4. For a detailed discussion of this poem see Finn Brandt-Petersen's analysis from a pedagogical point of view, "Benny Andersen: Hold op," _Modernisme og pædagogik_ (Copenhagen, 1966), pp. 84-93.

5. "Smile," _Selected Poems_, pp. 55/57; hereafter, translations from this edition are identified as _SP_ in the text.

6. Karl Marx, _The German Ideology_, Part I (London, 1970), p. 47.

7. Roland Barthes, _Mythologies_, pp. 140-141.

8. "Autonomous," _Selected Poems_, p. 71. From _Kamera med køkkenadgang_: "Nasseprins," p. 29: "Den Intellektuelle," p. 34; "Moralisten," p. 37; "Galan," p. 57. From _Portrætgalleri_ (Copenhagen, 1966): "Verdensmand," p. 30; "Den pæne mand," p. 40.

9. _Selected Poems_, p. 87.

10. _Kamera med køkkenadgang_, p. 36.

11. _Her i reservatet_ (Copenhagen, 1971), p. 13.

12. For a discussion of "Headliner" refer to ch. 2, sect. I.

13. "Vanskeligt tilfælde," _Her i reservatet_, p. 13. All translated quotations are based on this reference.

14. "Fredningsrapport," _Her i reservatet_, p. 9.

Chapter Four

1. Selected Poems, p. 107.

2. Ibid., p. 95.

3. Kamera med køkkenadgang, pp. 16-18.

4. Søren Kierkegaard's Journals and Papers, Ed. and Trans.   Howard V. Hong and Edna H. Hong (Bloomington-London, 1970), vol. 2, p. 529:No. 2276.

5. Jean-Paul Sartre, Nausea, trans. Robert Baldick (Harmondsworth, 1973), p. 113-114.

6. Steffen Hejlskov Larsen, "En spøgefuld pessimist," Lyriske tilværelsesmodeller (Copenhagen, 1968), pp. 126-128. Hejlskov Larsen also mentions that it is not unusual in Danish to use "lighthouse" as a nickname for a tall person.

7. This poems reflects the inspiration from the nursery rhyme "This Is the House that Jack Built"; see ch. 1, sect. II.

8. Jean-Paul Sartre, Existentialism and Human Emotions, pp. 56-57. In Andersen's poem "Tumling" from Det sidste øh (Copenhagen, 1969), pp. 20-21, both his theme and technique are demonstrated through the contrastive use of the active and passive forms of Danish verbs as a stylistic device for thematic emphasis; but it is impossible to render this technique into English with the same fluency and elegance because of a fundamental difference between English and Danish grammar.

9. Det sidste øh, p. 20.

10. "På afveje" ("Astray"), Den indre bowlerhat, p. 48.

11. "Livet" ("Life"), ibid., p. 25; in Danish, the expression "with body and soul" carries the double meaning "with life and soul."

12. "Til sommeren," Under begge øjne (Copenhagen, 1978), p. 32.

13. Existentialism and Human Emotions, p. 84.   Gunnar   Ekelöf, "Enkel är födelsen," Swedish Poetry , eds. Irene Scobbie and Philip Holmes (Stockholm-Hull, 1980), p. 112; in translation, the poem reads as follows: "Birth is simple: / You become you / Death is simple: / You are no longer you / It could have been the other way around / as in a mirror world: / Death could have born you / and life could have erased you / the one as well as the other-- / And perhaps it is like this: / From Death you have come, slowly / Life levels you." See also Torben Broström's analysis in Moderne svensk litteratur (Copenhagen, 1973), p. 130.

14. "Her hvor det ikke foregår," Personlige papirer (Copenhagen, 1974), p. 51.

15. See "Poetik," Swedish Poetry, p. 109; the translation of the poem's last five lines reads as follows: "And everything I so artfully try to write / is, by contrast, something artless / and all the fullness is empty / What I have written/ is written between the lines."

16. "Life Is Narrow and High," Selected Poems, p. 133.

17. In another but similar context, Bent Windfeld has hinted at a wrong attitude among people which guides their perception. "Hverdagsbilleder," Kristeligt Dagblad, December 5, 1964.

18. "Ironiens frygtløse distance," Analyser af moderne dansk lyrik 2, ed. Per Olsen (Copenhagen, 1976), pp. 82-97.

19. Ibid., pp. 95-97.

20. Alexander Taylor's translation in Selected Poems, p. 45, reads "spermatoza" here which must be a misprint; I have changed it to "spermatozoon" in accordance with the Danish original.

21. "Mandag," Her i reservatet, pp. 25-26.

22. "For Orientation," trans. Alexander Taylor, Seventeen Danish Poets (Lincoln, 1981), pp. 85/87. The translation contains a few inaccuracies; in my quotation, I have changed "Then I walked there in the night," to "There I walked in the night" in accordance with the Danish original in Under begge øjne, pp. 65-66.

23. Steffen Hejlskov Larsen uses this term to describe Andersen's technique of enumeration; "Alle gode gange tre," Lyriske tilværelsesmodeller, pp. 119-120.

24. See notes 13, 14, and 15 above. In "For Orientation," there is a clear affinity to Sartre's view that life must be given a meaning individually whereby the individual can participate in the creation of a human community; see Existentialism and Human Emotions, p. 49.

25. "Certain Days," Selected Poems, p. 79.

26. Ibid., p. 81.

27. "Den sejlivede strandvasker," which can be translated as "Washed Ashore," Portrætgalleri, p. 27.

28. See the discussion of the poems "Endure," and "The Stammering" in ch. 3, sect. I.

29. "Den søvnløse digter," Det sidste øh, p. 10.

Chapter Five

1. "På afveje," Den indre bowlerhat, 6th ed. (Copenhagen, 1967), p. 49.

2. "Synspunkt vedrørende klagesange," ("Viewpoint Regarding Complaints"), Personlige papirer, p. 22.

3. See above, ch. 4, note 23. The enumeration of three contrastive elements on the verbal level is thus given a parallel on the structural level through the juxtaposition of three contrasting states, and thereby a maximum of emphasis is achieved.

4. "Ad helvede til eller En selvplagers vej til fortabelse," ("To Hell or A Self-tormentor's Way to Perdition"), Personlige papirer, p. 61.

5. Ibid., p. 60.

6. "Man burde," ("You oughta"), Den indre bowlerhat, pp. 51-52. See also the description of similar efforts in "Sjælen," ("The Soul"), ibid., pp. 19-20.

7. Under begge øjne, pp. 35-37.

8. Ibid., pp. 25-26.

9. "To One Who Threw a Chair," trans. Alexander Taylor, Seventeen Danish Poets (Lincoln, 1981), pp. 81/83.

10. Himmelspræt eller Kunsten at komme til verden (Copenhagen, 1979), pp. 16-75.

11. Kamera med køkkenadgang, p. 55; for a fuller discussion, see ch. 3, sect. I.

12. "Alt," ("All"), Himmelspræt, p. 15.

13. "Himmelspræt" (Blanket-Toss"), Himmelspræt, pp. 16-19.

14. See Sartre, Nausea, pp. 182-193.

15. Although one can agree with Johannes Møllehave that being there for others is very important for being "et selv" (a self), it must also be stressed that Møllehave's statement is misleading when he equates the two by saying: "at være et selv, er at være til for et andet selv" (To be a self is to be there for another self). At the individual's level, there are far more dimensions to being "a self" than Møllehave's equation leads to believe. Læsehest med æselører. Oplevelser med danske bøger fra H.C. Andersen og Blicher til Benny Andersen og Lola Baidel. (Copenhagen, 1979), p. 242.

16.   Oven visse vande (Above Certain Waters), (Copenhagen, 1981): See the songs "Hilsen til forårssolen" ("Greetings to the Spring Sun"), "Da jeg mødte dig" ("When I met you"), "Rosalina."

17.   "Mose," Portrætgalleri, p. 56.   "Kærligheden," Den indre bowlerhat, p. 30.

18.   Kierkegaard, Either/Or, trans. Walter Lowrie (New York, 1959), p. 173.   Also Sartre stresses the necessity of the choice; in view of the absence of general directives for a correct choice, he emphasizes the responsible choice. Existentialism and Human Emotions, 52-59.

19.   For a detailed analysis, see ch. 2, sect. II.

Chapter Six

1. In his essay "Velfærdsstat og personlighed," (1956; "Welfare State and Personality"), the writer and philosopher Villy Sørensen had already called attention to this other reality when he warned the individual of suspending the development of the personality by repressing existential fears and merely seeking refuge in economic and social security. Digtere og dæmoner , 2nd ed. (Copenhagen, 1979), pp. 219-227.

2. Lars Grahn, in "Dansk välfärdsabsurdism," BLM 8(1969), pp. 632-633.

3. Benny Andersen, Puderne, 2nd ed. (Copenhagen, 1965), pp. 12-13. All page references in the text are to this edition.

4. For a fuller discussion of the poem, refer to ch. 3, sect. I.

5. Both "livet" ("Life") and "På afveje" ("Astray") emphasize the necessity of active involvement: Den indre bowlerhat, pp. 25 and 47-50 respectively.

6. This situation is reminiscent of Camus' description of beginning consciousness when "it happens that the stage sets collapse" all of a sudden. The Myth of Sisyphus, trans. Justin O'Brien (New York, 1957), p. 12. In contemporary Danish literature, Peter Seeberg's short stories often focus on the situation described.

7. Benny Andersen, "The Passage," trans. Paula Hostrup-Jessen, The Devil's Instrument, ed. Sven Holm (London, 1971), pp. 255-256.

8. Ibid., p. 260

9. Introduction to The Devil's Instrument, p. 9.

10. "The Passage," The Devil's Instrument, p. 249.

11. Sartre, Nausea, p. 115.

12. R. D. Laing, The Divided Self (Harmondsworth, 1965). Preface to the Pelican edition.

13. Carlos Fuentes, "Writing in Time," a lecture given in the Humanities Lecture Series at the University of Kansas, December 1, 1980. Cf. also a play, such as Ibsen's Ghosts.

14. Benny Andersen, "Puderne," Puderne, pp. 150-151.

15. Benny Andersen, "Et lykkeligt menneske," ("A Happy Person"), Tykke-Olsen m.fl., 4th ed. (Copenhagen, 1969), pp. 171-78. All subsequent page references in the text are to this edition.

16. See F. M. Dostoevsky, "Notes from the Underground," The Best Short Stories of Dostoevsky, trans. David Magarshack (New York, 1955), p. 250.

17. Søren Kierkegaard, The Concept of Dread, trans. Walter Lowrie, 2nd ed. (Princeton, 1966), p. 106.

18. Jean-Paul Sartre, Existentialism and Human Emotions, p. 93.

19. R. D. Laing, The Divided Self, p. 25.

Chapter Seven

1. Lars Grahn, "Staten har blivit sjukantig. Ingen tar någon notis om det," Göteborgs Handels- och Sjöfartstidning, September 17, 1969.

2. "Tykke-Olsen," Tykke Olsen m.fl., 4th ed. (Copenhagen, 1969), pp. 33-65. All page references in the text are to this edition. Alexander Taylor assisted with this translation.

3. Stig Krabbe Barfoed, "Ny Benny Andersen-noveller," Aalborg Stiftstidende, October 19, 1968.

4. Ibid.

Chapter Eight

1. See ch. 6, sect. V.

2. See, e.g., Sven Bedsted, "Benny Andersens barokke banaliteter," Jyllands-Posten, October 6, 1972; Steffen Hejlskov Larsen, "Benny Andersens Sjov i Danmark," Weekendavisen, June 21, 1974.

3. Benny Andersen, Svantes viser, 13th ed. (Copenhagen, 1980), p. 65. All page references in the text are to this edition.

4. See, e.g., Stig Krabbe Barfoed's criticism of the collection Tykke-olsen m. fl. because Andersen presents a diagnosis here "without suggestions for treatment" of the disease. "Ny Benny Andersen-noveller," Aalborg Stiftstidende, October 19, 1968.

5. Jean-Paul Sartre, Nausea, p. 248.

6. Ibid., p. 248-249.

7. Benny Andersen, På broen (Copenhagen, 1981), p. 28.

8. See ch. 1, sect. I, as well as chronology.

9. Benny Andersen, På broen, pp. 239-240.

10. For a critical introduction to the works of H. C. Branner, the reader is referred to T. L. Markey, H. C. Branner, TWAS 245 (New York, 1973).

11. Benny Andersen, Undskyld hr.-hvor ligger naturen? (Copenhagen, 1973), Excuse me, Sir-where Is Nature?. Snøvs is the main character of the other three novels for children: Snøvsen og Eigil og katten i sækken (Snøvs, and Eigil and the Cat in the Bag; the cat in the bag, one of the characters of the book, is derived from an idiom which corresponds to the English expression "the pig in the poke." (Copenhagen, 1967). Snøvsen på sommerferie (Snøvs on Summer Vacation), (Copenhagen, 1970). Snøvsen og Snøvsine (Snøvs and his Girl friend Snøvsine), (Copenhagen, 1972). The three volumes dealing with snøvs will be referred to as the Snøvsen-trilogy and quotations will refer to the volumes as I, II, III respectively, followed by page numbers that refer to the editions above. Because snøvs is derived from an idiom, the name will not be capitalized; this is in agreement with the Danish original.

12. Undskyld hr. - hvor ligger naturen?, p. 23.

13. Roland Barthes, "Myth Today," Mythologies, p. 109-159; see also ch. 2, sect. II.

14. This can be seen especially in <u>Her i reservatet</u> and in <u>Orfeus i undergrunden</u>.

15. "Possibilities," <u>Den musikalske ål</u>, p. 65.

Chapter Nine

1. Antologi af nordisk litteratur, 2nd ed. vol. 11,   eds. Sigurd
Kværndrup, Hansjørgen Nielsen,   and Ebbe Sønderiis (Copenhagen,
1971), pp. 465, 477.

2. Finn Stein Larsen,   "Lyrik," Modernismen i dansk litteratur,
ed. Jørn Vosmar (Copenhagen, 1969), p. 55.

3. Søren Baggesen, "Prosa," Modernismen i dansk litteratur , p.
130; Baggesen does not include Benny Andersen's stories in his
overview.

4. Andersen in his interview "En lystig alvorsmand og alvorlig
humorist," Vestjysk Aktuelt, Feb. 20, 1967; see also Andersen's
remarks in his interview with Jens Henneberg, "Jeg er ikke entydig
humorist," Aalborg Stiftstidende, March 1, 1967.

5. See Søren Kierkegaard,   The Point of View for my Work as an
Author, trans. Walter Lowrie (New York: Harper, 1962).

6. In the case of the poem "It's High Time," Keld Zeruneith has
pointed out how easily the reader might feel superior to the
speaker in the poem, and might even ridicule him thus missing the
critical dimension of the poem. "Ironiens frygtløse distance,"
Analyser af moderne dansk lyrik 2, ed. Per Olsen (Copenhagen,
1967), pp. 96-97.

7. Niels Barfoed, "Et, du er den!" Politiken, October 9, 1966.

Selected Bibliography

Primary Sources

1. Poetry

Den indre bowlerhat. Copenhagen: Borgen, 1964. 6th ed., 1967.

Den musikalske ål. Copenhagen: Borgen, 1960.

Det sidste øh. Copenhagen: Borgen, 1969.

Her i reservatet. Copenhagen: Borgen, 1971.

Himmelspræt eller Kunsten at komme til verden.   Copenhagen:
    Borgen, 1979.

Kamera med køkkenadgang. Copenhagen: Borgen, 1962; 3rd ed.,
    1965.

Man burde burde. Udvalgte digte, ed. Niels Barfoed. Copenhagen:
    Borgen, 1971.

Personlige papirer. Copenhagen: Borgen, 1974.

Portrætgalleri. Copenhagen: Borgen, 1966.

Under begge øjne. Copenhagen: Borgen, 1978.

2.   Other Poems in Journals and Anthologies

Det ny notat, December 1, 1978: "Danmark--et broget fore-
tagende."

Heretica, 1952: "Ny luft," p. 264; 1953: "Dronningens elsker,"
pp. 32-37, "Sten," p. 287, "Vi får øjnene tilbage," p. 289.

Hvedekorn, 1960: "Auktion," p. 39, "Den skrigende stad," pp.
39-40; 1961: "I sommervarmen," p. 93, "Under vægten af
drømme," pp. 91-92.

I granneland, "Jeg ved lidt om Norge." Oslo: Cappelen, 1981, p.
46.

Kvinderne og freden, "Ordet fred." Copenhagen: Aros, 1980, pp.
64-65.

Ord om Vietnam. En internasjonal antologi, "Kæmperne."   Oslo:
Gyldendal, 1967, pp. 11-13.

Selvsyn, "Udkast til tidsportræt, 1962/63, 1, pp. 28-29.

Undervands-Tidende: Vigtige digte!, "Fortids fremtid," pp.
35-37 and "Andrew Young og afgrunden," pp. 245-46. Copenhagen: Tiderne Skifter, 1979.

3.   Fiction

Puderne. Copenhagen: Borgen, 1965. Short stories.

På broen. Copenhagen: Borgen, 1981. Novel.

Tykke-Olsen m. fl.. Copenhagen: Borgen, 1968. 4th ed., 1969.
Short stories.

Svantes viser. En sanghistorie. Copenhagen: Borgen, 1972.
13th ed., 1980. Tale with interspersed poems set to music.

4.   Plays

En lykkelig skilsmisse. Film script with Henning Carlsen.
Copenhagen: Borgen, 1975.

Kolde fødder. Copenhagen: Rhodos, 1980.

Nomader med noder. Digte og erindringer. Copenhagen: Borgen, 1976. Poems and reminiscences.

"Notater om inspiration." In: Det danske akademi 1975-81. Copenhagen: Gyldendal, 1981.

Oven visse vande. En sangbog. Songbook and record with Povl Dissing. Copenhagen: Borgen, 1981.

Svantes viser. Record with Povl Dissing. Copenhagen, 1973.

7. Works in English Translation

A Bibliography of Danish Literature in English Translation 1950-1980. With a Selection of Books about Denmark. Comp. Carol L. Schroeder. Copenhagen: Det danske Selskab, 1982, pp. 23-26. Lists works by and about B. Andersen.

Contemporary Danish Poetry. An Anthology, eds. Line Jensen, Erik Vagn Jensen, Knud Mogensen, Ale Copenhagen: Gyldendal and Boston: Twayne, 1977, pp. 242- 249: "This Uncertainty," "Goodness," "M," "Photographs," "Time," "Life Is Narrow and High," "Earthworm," "High and Dry," "Melancholy," "A Hole in the Earth," trans. Alexander Taylor.

Modern Scandinavian Poetry 1900-1975, ed. Martin Allwood. Mullsjo/Sweden: Anglo-America Center, 1982, pp. 128-130: "On Terra Firma," "Suck," "Sound sleeper," "The same," "The memories," trans. Martin Allwood and Robert Lyng.

Mundus Artium, vol. 5, 1/2(1972): "The Pants," trans. Hanne Gliese-Lee, pp. 44-51; vol. 8,2 (1975): "Hiccups," trans. Leonie A. Marx, pp. 30-32.

Prism International, vol. 12,1 (1973): "The Intellectual," trans. Hanne Gliese-Lee, p. 96.

Scandinavian Review, vol. 67,2 (1979): "To a Strong Woman," trans. Nadia Christensen, p. 17; "Family Idyl," trans. Alexander Taylor, p. 16.

Scanorama. The Magazine of SAS, vol. 6,4 (1977): "The Hiccups," trans. Richard J. Litell, pp. 42-43.

Selected Poems, trans. Alexander Taylor, Princeton: Princeton University Press, 1975. So far the most representative selection from Andersen's first seven volumes of poetry; available in a bilingual and in an English paperback edition.

Selected Stories, ed. Leonie Marx, Willimantic: Curbstone Press, 1983. A selection from Andersen's two volumes of short stories, a chapter from his novel På broen, and a critical introduction to his works.

Seventeen Danish Poets, ed. Niels Ingwersen, Lincoln: Windflower Press, 1981, pp. 80-89: "To One Who Threw a Chair,"
"To SAS," "For Orientation," "Such a Morning," trans. Alexander Taylor. Bilingual.

The Devil's Instrument, ed. Sven Holm, London: Owen, 1971, pp.
247-260: "The Passage," trans. Paula Hostrup-Jessen.

The Evergreen Review, vol. 41 (1966): "Tarzan. The Government.
Refrigerators," trans. Ken Tindall, pp. 42-45; reprinted in
Evergreen Review Reader, ed. Barney Rosset. New York: Grove
Press, 1968, pp. 750-753.

The Malahat Review, vol. 32 (1974): "Layer Cake," trans. Hanne
Gliese-Lee; vol. 52 (1979): "The Drowning," trans. Elin El-
gaard, pp. 28-40.

Translation, vol. IX(1982): "Compassion," "Heart in   Snow,"
"Sponge Prince," trans. Alexander Taylor, pp. 3-5.

                    Secondary Sources

Andersen, Hans. "Gør det forbudte," Jyllands-Posten, October 3,
    1965.   Interview with Benny Andersen about aspects of his
    works.

Antologi af nordisk litteratur 1960-1973. Kværndrup, Hansjørgen
    Nielsen, and Ebbe Sønderiis. 2nd ed., vol. 11. Copenhagen:
    Samleren, 1976. Brief discussion of Andersen's position in
    contemporary Danish literature, pp. 465, 467.

Barfoed, Niels. "At indvinde ny svimmelhed," Politiken, Sep-
    tember 23, 1969. Review of The Last Er.

_____. "Benny Andersen. Den musikalske ål," Vindrosen 7
    (1960), p. 586. Review of The Musical Eel.

_____. "Et, du er den!," Politiken, October 9, 1966.   Review
    of Portrait Gallery.

_____. "Særling i forstaden," Politiken, May 21, 1971.
    Review of the TV-film version of the story of "Fats Olsen."

Barfoed, Stig Krabbe. "Ny Benny Andersen-noveller," Aal-
    borg Stiftstidende.   October 19, 1968. Review of Fats Olsen
    and Other Stories.

Bedsted, Sven. "Bennys barokke banaliteter," Jyllands-Posten,
    November 2, 1962. Review of Camera with Kitchen Privileges.

Brandt, Jørgen Gustava. Præsentation. Copenhagen: Gyldendal,
    1964. Brief general introduction to Andersen's works.

Lejemorderen og andre spil. Copenhagen: Borgen, 1970.   Plays
    for radio and TV.

Man sku' være noget ved musikken. Film script with Henning Carl-
    sen. Copenhagen, 1972.

Orfeus i undergrunden. Copenhagen: Borgen, 1979.   Adapted for
    film with Dan Tschernia, under the title Danmark er lukket,
    1980; unpublished manuscript.

Snak. In: Moderne Dansk dramatisk I, ed. Chr. Ludvigsen. Copen-
    hagen: Arena, 1966.

5. Children's Books

Den hæse drage. Børnekomedie. Copenhagen: Borgen, 1969.   Book
    and record.

Lille Peter Dille og andre udenlandske børnerim og remser. Copen-
    hagen: Borgen, 1964. Collection of foreign nursery rhymes.

Nikke Nikke Nambo og andre danske børnerim og remser. Copenhagen:
    Borgen, 1963. Collection of Danish nursery rhymes.

Snøvsen og Eigil og katten i sækken. Copenhagen: Borgen, 1967.

Snøvsen på sommerferie. Copenhagen: Borgen, 1970.

Snøvsen og Snøvsine. Copenhagen: Borgen, 1972.

Undskyld hr., hvor ligger naturen? Børnelytterroman. Copenhagen:
    Borgen, 1973. A radio novel.

6. Miscellaneous

Barnet der blev ældre og ældre. Kronikker og erindringer. Copen-
    hagen: Borgen, 1973. Essays and reminiscences.

Benny Andersen læser Benny Andersen. Copenhagen, 1965. Record.

"Børns sprog og børns oplevelse af sproget." In:
    Det danske akademi: En bog om sproget 1967-74." Copenhagen:
    Gyldendal, 1974, pp. 40-48. Essay on children's language and
    children's experiences with language.

"Da Danmark blev nedlagt." In: Viktor B. Andersens Maskinfabrik,
    5(1976); reprinted in: Danmark og danskere, ed. Thorkild
    Borup Jensen. Copenhagen: Gyldendal, 1979, pp. 48-50.
    Story, thematically linked with the play Or-
    feus i Undergrunden, for which it served as model.

Brandt-Petersen, Finn. "Benny Andersen 'Hold op,'" Modernisme og
    pædagogik. Copenhagen: Glydendal, 1966, pp. 84-93.
    Analysis of the poem "Hold op" ("Stop"), from a pedagogical
    point of view.

_____. "Den intellektuelle," Tekstlæsning. Copenhagen: Gyl-
    dendal, 1967, pp. 91-92. Analysis of the poem "The Intellec-
    tual."

Brostrøm, Torben. "Andersens sult," Information, December 8,
    1971. Review of Anthology Man burde burde (You oughta
    oughta).

_____. "B. Svante Andersens harpe," Information, October 5,
    1972. Review of Svante's Songs.

_____. Introduction to Contemporary Danish Poetry. An An-
    thology, eds. Line Jensen, Erik Vagn Jensen, Knud Mogensen,
    and Alexander D. Taylor. Copenhagen: Gyldendal and Boston:
    Twayne, 1977, pp. 1-10. Useful, short survey of the charac-
    teristics and the heritage of contemporary Danish poetry.

_____ and Jens Kistrup. Dansk litteraturhistorie. 3rd ed.,
    vol. 4. Copenhagen: Politikens Forlag, 1971. General sur-
    vey of modern Danish literature; Andersen's works are
    discussed on pp. 406, 376-380, 398, 576-577; in the aug-
    mented and updated edition of Dansk litteratur historie, vol.
    6, Andersen's works are discussed on pp. 151-160 and 376-77.

_____. "Den ny underfladepoesi," Information, September 23,
    1969. Review of The Last Er.

_____, ed. Opgøret med modernismen. Copenhagen: Tabula/
    Fremad, 1974. A collection of critical articles on the
    various phases of Danish Modernism.

_____, Moderne svensk litteratur. Copenhagen: Chr. Ejler,
    1973. A history of modern Swedish literature, 1940-72.

_____. Ti års lyrik, Copenhagen: Gyldendal, 1966. Contains
    reviews of The Musical Eel, and Camera with Kitchen
    Privileges, pp. 183-188.

"En lystig alvorsmand og alvorlig humorist," Vestjysk Aktuelt,
    Feb. 20, 1967.

Franzén, lars Olof. Punktnedslag i dansk litteratur 1880-1970.
    Copenhagen: Lindhardt and Ringhof, 1971. Andersen's early
    poetry and fiction are commented on in the context of Danish
    literature, pp. 141-147.

Grahn, Lars. "Dansk välfärdsabsurdism," BLM 8 (1969), pp.
    632-633. Review of The Pillows.

_____. "Staten har blivit sjukantig.. Ingen tar någon notis
om det," Göteborgs Handels- och Sjöfartstidning, September
17, 1969. Review of Fats Olsen and Other Stories.

Henneberg, Jens. "Jeg er ikke entydig humorist," Aalborg
Stiftstidende, March 1, 1967.

Jensen, Thorkild Borup. "Benny Andersen." In: Danske Digtere i
det 20. Århundrede, eds. Frederik Nielsen and Ole Restrup.
Vol 3. Copenhagen: Gad, 1966, pp. 677-691. An extensive
discussion of Andersen's works.

Knudsen, Jørgen. "Udbrændt specialist?" Højskolebladet, Nr. 50
(1968) pp. 834-836. Review of Fats Olsen and Other Stories.

Kristensen, Tom. Fra Holger Drachmann til Benny Andersen. Copenhagen: Gyldendal, 1967. Reviews of Danish poetry.

_____. "Fra musikalsk til elektrisk ål," Politiken, November
24, 1962. Review of Camera with Kitchen Privileges.

Kromann, Jette. Digtere på band. Vol. 1. Copenhagen: Borgen, 1966. Interview with Andersen on pp. 7-46.

Kruuse, Jens. "Det stilfærdige oprør," Jyllands-Posten, November
5, 1965. Review of The Pillows.

Larsen, Steffen Hejlskov. "Benny Andersens Sjov i Danmark,"
Weekendavisen, June 21, 1974. Review of Svante's Songs.

_____. Lyriske tilværelsesmodeller. Copenhagen: Borgen,
1968. Contains the interpretations of the poems "Man burde"
("You oughta") and "High and Dry."

_____. "Om billedstrukturer i dansk lyrik," Danske Studier 61
(1966), pp. 5-45. Discusses imagery in 19th and 20th century
Danish poetry, and mentions Andersen very briefly in this
context.

Marx, Leonie. "Benny Andersen." In Encyclopedia of World Literature in the 20th Century. 2nd revised and enlarged ed.,
vol. 1. New York: Ungar, 1981, pp. 83-84. General introduction to Andersen's works.

_____. "Exercises in Living: Benny Andersen's Literary
Perspectives," World Literature Today 52,4 (1978), pp.
550-554. General presentation with specific analyses of the
poems "Goodness," "Smile," "Widescreen," "Time," and the
story "The Passage;" expanded versions of these interpretations are incorporated in this monograph.

Mitchell, P. M. A History of Danish Literature. 2nd augmented
ed. New York: Kraus-Thomson, 1971. General survey with a
brief comment on Andersen's early poetry, p. 313.

Mølbjerg, Hans. "Et korrektiv til nærlæsning af ny lyrik." Meddelelser fra Dansklærerforeningen 3(1968), pp. 162-174. Contains an analysis of the poem "Hold op" ("Stop"), pp. 172-174.

Møllehave, Johannes. Læsehest med æseløer. Oplevelser med danske bøger fra H. C. Andersen og Blicher til Benny Andersen og Lola Baidel. Copenhagen: Lindhardt og Ringhof, 1979, pp. 228-242. Contains a chapter, "På afveje," with Møllehaves impressions of and reactions to Benny Andersen's works.

Storm, Ole. "Sådan forulemper man," Politiken, November 2, 1965. Review of The Pillows.

Vosmar, Jørn, ed. Modernismen i dansk litteratur. Copenhagen: Fremad 1969. Contains a discussion of Andersen's early poetry in Finn Stein Larsen's section "Lyrik," (pp. 45, 47, 55-56,101-102, 117) and a brief mention in Søren Baggesen's section on "Prosa," (p. 188).

Zern, Leif. "Benny Andersen," Komma, 2 (1966), pp. 22-23. General introduction for Swedish readers.

Zeruneith, Keld. "Ironiens frygtløse distance." Analyser af moderne dansk lyrik 2, ed. Per Olsen. Copenhagen: Borgen, 1976, pp. 82-97. Thematic and structural analysis of the poem "It's High Time" with special attention given to the use of irony.

Index